SELL TO WIN

10 PRINCIPLES TO ACHIEVE SALES EXCELLENCE

TIM GALLAGHER

Editing, design, distribution by Bublish

Published by Tim Gallagher

ISBN: 978-1-64704-986-7 (eBook)
ISBN: 978-1-64704-987-4 (paperback)
ISBN: 978-1-64704-988-1 (hardcover)

To Sandy, who supported me every step of the journey.

.

Contents

Introduction

You are in it to win it—*Sell to Win!*

Every day competitors are trying to take your business. Your customers must believe that you and the company you work for create a competitive advantage for them in their business. The sales skills you bring to the important work you do are what differentiate you from everyone else.

Are you a top sales performer in your industry, or are you getting by with just enough effort to make a living? Professional selling is not a passive job where you show up and someone tells you what to do. A sales career is a competitive journey where you need to have a *process* to win consistently. Selling is a long-term endeavor built on your commitment to your job, the value you bring to customers, and the relationships you build along the way. This book is for people who are enthusiastic about their sales career and motivated to get better results.

Great salespeople can move mountains for their companies. They are the bridge between the company they work for and precious customers. A great sales representative creates a superior customer experience that can lead to long-lasting and profitable business relationships.

This book is the advice I would have given myself forty years ago when I started my sales career. Now it is the insight I want to share to help you be successful in sales. I always viewed my sales career as a competition and a game I wanted to win. I admit it. I needed to win, and it was not optional. For me winning is personal. I needed not only the money to support my family but also the victories because second place has never been comfortable. If you are a competitive person, you feel the same way. I have always admired great competitors: people who have the persistence, courage, and humility to always be improving. I never met a successful sales pro who was not extremely competitive.

Sell to Win is about how applying key principles can differentiate you from everyone else and enable you to win *consistently*. When you win in sales, you gain business, make yourself valuable within your organization, and make more money. It would have been great to have had a guide to reference as I was starting and navigating the challenges in my sales career. This book will speed up the success curve for you. It is difficult to have consistent, outstanding performance in a sales career. Sales is a demanding profession that will challenge you but also prove to be extremely rewarding.

Competing in sales is about finding a strategic advantage and using it to tip the odds of success in your favor. In my career, I had some great wins but also had my share of disappointments. There were times when I thought a sale should have gone my way but did not. No one wins every time, but we need to make sure we have the skills to win *most* of the time. I have worked with many outstanding sales pros, and none were exactly alike. The best pros find a way to put their authentic personal stamp on their sales strategy. Everyone sells differently, but there are key principles that the best follow consistently.

* * *

I started in field sales a long time ago and had progressive sales management positions culminating in overseeing a sales organization of a hundred people. In the last decade, our sales team exceeded our annual sales budget and grew our sales and market share, in a consistently declining market. This was the result of tremendous efforts by the folks who made our products and sales pros who brought the value story to our customers. I have learned so much from working in and leading sales teams over many years. Four decades of experience and collaborating with outstanding people have provided me with a great perspective on what it takes to win in sales. In my career, I logged more than four thousand customer visits. Many sales calls were effective, and others I am sure could have been improved on.

As a sales manager working with great sales pros, I learned that the best separate themselves by consistently being better at applying the disciplines of selling. Traveling with excellent salespeople provided a unique perspective on how to connect with customers. I have distilled the essential principles that separate top performers from the rest.

Whether you are a seasoned pro looking to refine your approach or a newcomer eager to make your mark, this book will equip you with the tools and strategies to consistently exceed your goals.

Are you ready to learn the key sales insights that will help you stand out? Let's get started on the road to *Sell to Win*!

About This Book

If you don't play to win, don't play at all.

—*Tom Brady*

WHY ANOTHER SALES BOOK?

Too many people enter the sales profession without the foundational knowledge of what selling is about. Hiring someone into sales and wishing them success is not a great recipe for sustainable performance. Sales success is built around key principles that lay the foundation of professional effectiveness. Understanding customers and helping them solve complex problems takes time and training.

With my diploma in hand on college graduation day decades ago, I had no idea what I wanted to do for work.

My dad, in his classic one-liner way, said, "Tim, you should get into sales." I responded, "Sales? What is that?" For me, forty years later, the rest is history. My mission after graduation was to interview for sales positions with every company that would talk with me. I was determined to get a job in sales and prove I could be effective.

Sell to Win is a strategic guide to consistently excelling in sales by applying universal principles. Steadily practicing these principles will give you a significant edge to be a top performer. This book will focus on the personal strategic principles of sales success and not the tactics of the actual sales call. Sales call tactics and the customer buying cycle are topics for another book. The information that follows is designed to empower both experienced professionals and those new to selling with the necessary knowledge, insight, and tools to thrive in today's competitive market. Regardless of where you are in your career, you will find valuable insights on these pages. The advice here stems from decades of experience in sales, leading sales teams, learning from exceptional salespeople, and collaborating with remarkable customers. Every day, you are vying for your customer's business, and you need to outshine the competition. If you are in the game, aim to win. I am excited to share the essential insights that will help you reach your sales objectives and make you one of the best.

Here is what we will cover:

- Building your personal foundation for success.

- Reviewing the ten key "Sales Separators."

- Over a hundred helpful ideas you can start using now.

- Your action plans for improvement.

Whether you aim to increase your income, advance your career, or simply enhance your sales skills, this book offers the guidance you need to reach your full potential. This is an interactive workbook, including many questions for your input and space for your notes. I hope you write all over this book, making your notes a valuable reference for the future.

The Best Job in the World

The only way to do great work
is to love what you do.

—*Steve Jobs*

Are you fired up to be in sales? Sales is an incredible career and one of the best jobs in the world. I discovered this when I got my first sales territory. At twenty-four, I was driving an old station wagon provided by my company, enjoying the freedom of the road, building great relationships, making sales, and earning good money. I would often find myself thinking, *They are paying me for this?* It was exciting to be on the road, challenging myself to grow my territory.

My first sales position was selling and servicing products for a chemical company to manufacturing operations. It was a great learning opportunity as I started my sales career. It was amazing to be collaborating with different customers and pursuing new business opportunities. I was on the road, had an expense account, and had complete control of my schedule. It was incredible to be helping customers and growing my business. I was full of enthusiasm and wanted to prove I could be successful in sales.

The excitement of pursuing and securing new business still thrills me. By choosing this career path, you have opened the door to a life of challenge and growth. You should be excited to be in sales! You represent everything about your company to the customer. You are the tip of the spear for your organization when dealing with precious customers.

Sales offers a unique opportunity for autonomy, relationship building, and increased income. A sales career allows you to compete for business and measure your performance. It is fulfilling to solve problems for people and offer value-added solutions. As often noted, everyone dabbles in sales in some way, whether it is instilling values in our children or pitching an idea at work. We are all playing the sales game. While you will inevitably face challenges, the rewards far surpass the obstacles. The enthusiasm you bring to your sales role will set the stage for your success.

I truly hope you find your career in sales exciting, challenging, and immensely rewarding. Congratulations on having one of the best jobs in the world. Skilled salespeople are always in demand. Our economy thrives on individuals who can solve problems, foster relationships, and grow business.

Now, let's look at what separates the best.

What Separates the Best?

> *Motivation is what gets you started;*
> *habit is what keeps you going.*
>
> —*Jim Rohn*

WHAT SETS THE BEST APART?

Great salespeople are in for the long haul. They do not sell
for short-term gain but look to build lasting relationships
with customers that continue to grow over time. They run
the sales marathon, slow and steady. The best have a *process* to compete and win in their industry. I would define a
top sales performer as someone who *consistently exceeds*
their sales quota and *grows* their territory and annual
revenue. Top sales pros are highly motivated, disciplined,

and strategic and care deeply about helping their customers win. What distinguishes the top sales performers in your industry? It is not just luck or talent; it is a blend of skills, mindset, and strategies that makes them stand out. I have always paid close attention to great salespeople at work. From the business owner who hired me for my first sales job after college to some of my most important career mentors, I carefully observed what made them so effective.

Consider your favorite athletes, musicians, or entrepreneurs. What qualities do they possess that make them rise above everyone else? They have identified their unique strengths and used them to achieve extraordinary results. The best are hungry to win, have high expectations, and put in the work. They are always learning, reaching higher, and improving their skills. I always enjoyed watching Roger Federer's coolness in a tennis match, Tom Brady's determination with a minute left in the game, and Tiger Woods on the final day of a golf tournament. They had the talent and the system, and, most of all, they loved what they did. They were also never satisfied. The same applies in sales. In any competitive field, the best are never satisfied with the status quo. They constantly strive to improve to be the best at what they do.

In a study conducted by Steven W. Martin for the *Harvard Business Review*, he notes that salespeople who exceed their quota have what he refers to as verbal acuity: "This refers to a communication level where the meaning, nature, and importance of the words spoken by the salesperson are personally understood by the customer."[1] He also found that "Eighty-four percent of the top performers scored very high in achievement orientation."[2] Effective salespeople communicate well, set goals, and achieve them. A third key finding was that they had situational dominance. "Situational dominance is a personal interaction strategy by which the customer accepts the salesperson's recommendations and follows his advice."[3] Sales pros know their products and are confident in their recommendations.

CONSISTENT EFFORT OVER TIME WINS THE RACE

Consistency in our daily habits and actions is crucial to sustainable success. What we do every day is what defines us. Winners are consistent in their preparation, training, and business habits. How diligent are you with your sales planning, preparation, follow-up, and maintaining relationships? The best use a process and stay with it every day. This takes determination. Great competitors have incredible determination, courage, and perseverance. In the book *The Attributes,* Rich Diviney writes, "If courage is the ability to effectively move through fear, challenge, and discomfort, perseverance is the ability to keep doing it over and over again."[4] The best stay after it, always.

In my career, I found that if I worked consistently, pushing forward day after day, positive results eventually emerged. I figured if I helped people and was reliable, they would want to do business with me. This applied to how I conducted every facet of my business. I believed if I made the sales calls, followed up immediately, and was there when customers needed me, my sales would grow. My customers needed to have confidence that I would be there for them. When you consistently put in the work, results follow your efforts.

IT TAKES DISCIPLINE

To be the best at anything requires self-discipline, and professional selling is no different. Pros who are organized, plan well, and take care of their customers do it every day. They do not wait to be told what to do; they work proactively. In the classic book, *The 7 Habits of Highly Effective People* by Stephen R. Covey, the first habit in the book is "Be Proactive." Covey states, "The power to make and keep commitments to ourselves is the essence of developing the basic habits of effectiveness."[5] Keeping commitments requires discipline. The best sales pros make sure yesterday's business is finished and practice discipline in their daily professional habits. Expense reports, follow-up, and thoughtful account planning are just a few of the tasks that need to be done on time, every time. I had excellent managers throughout my career who strongly reinforced the need to honor my commitments. To quote one of my most influential mentors, "Do what you said you were going to do." He held me accountable to this all the time, and I did not want to disappoint him. His expectation never wavered.

When I reflect on the success that came my way, I believe part of it was the quality and frequency of the interactions I had with customers. How often I saw key contacts and my proximity to them were vital. Being geographically close to my major accounts enabled me to see my main contacts regularly and respond quickly to their needs. I needed to be disciplined with my schedule and make sure I was allocating my time wisely. Spending time with customers outside work was also important to my effectiveness. People need to know how much you care, and having a consistent and regular presence is essential. You need to be your customers' go-to person in the business you are in. High-frequency contact where you can forge a great relationship and bring value to their business is key. Your skills need to be visible to the right customers on a regular basis.

In the following chapters, we will explore the key principles that set top salespeople apart. These Separators are essential for building a successful and sustainable sales career. By applying these principles, you will gain a competitive edge and position yourself for long-term success.

We all need to find a strategic advantage when competing in anything. In sales, this can mean technical skills, relationships, presentation skills, or something else that sets you apart. The best salespeople have something unique that helps them win consistently. As we explore the principles that follow, the goal is to identify strategic advantages that can help you win. Everyone has a different approach to how they sell. You need to put your own authentic style to work for you so it comes naturally. When it comes naturally, it is sustainable.

But first, let's start with you.

It All Starts with You

> *First, take responsibility for your life, and second, take initiative. It's that simple. Be an agent, not a victim. Don't wait for life to happen to you, happen to it. Be the driver of your life, not the passenger. Live out of your imagination, not your past.*
>
> —Stephen R. Covey

MOTIVATION IS ESSENTIAL

What drives and motivates you? Do closing sales, earning recognition as a top performer, and making more money sound appealing? Ultimately, *you are in charge of your own success*. The energy and attitude you bring to work every day are the springboards to accomplishing your goals. No one can convince you to work hard and strive for excellence; this is a personal decision you must make if you want to stand out as a top sales performer. Many people claim they want to be successful, but do they have the desire, determination, and detailed plans to achieve it?

As a sales professional, you need to be highly motivated to stand out among everyone else in your industry. Motivation in a sales career cannot be overemphasized and is the starting point of effectiveness. People who succeed exert their positive energy consistently with customers and their company throughout their careers. Everyone is different, but all great salespeople care deeply about their customers.

I worked with professionals who had different skill sets, but all the best had an overwhelming desire to win. When we hired new people on our teams, we looked for candidates who had something to prove. Our goal was to hire people who had the desire to showcase their skills and provide value to customers. Great sales professionals are not comfortable with the status quo; they need to be growing their business all the time. This is the intensity you will need to stand out. As you look at your sales career, are you highly motivated to put in the work to win?

A *Harvard Business Review* study by Ryan Fuller entitled "3 Behaviors That Drive Successful Salespeople" examined what differentiates top sales performers from others in organizations. The study focused on three main behaviors that separated the top performers. The first one mentioned in the study is "Spending enough time with customers and prospects."[6] As expected, sales call frequency was key. The second finding was that "Having a large and healthy network in your organization."[7] was important. And finally, the third was "Spending time with and getting attention from your manager and other senior people in your organization."[8] Interesting that two of the three behaviors highlighted the importance of internal relationships. The study reinforces the importance of high customer interaction and building relationships internally. You need to have a lot of contact with people whether they are customers or your company. Your success will depend on working with many different people.

I always ask candidates in interviews about their core values. This helps uncover their true character. I want to know if they possess the commitment, discipline, and grit to succeed long term in sales. This is often referred to as mental toughness. When you believe your work is important and valued, it is incredible what can be accomplished.

Documenting our core values is a great starting point in understanding what is truly important to each of us. These values are at the heart of what brings meaning to our lives. Just as companies have core values that set the tone for their culture, we need our own to define what truly matters to us. Core values such as commitment, respect, integrity, and balance are some examples. A great management mentor of mine always asked me when we were hiring someone, "Will the candidate fit into our culture?" He believed in hiring people who fit our values first and then for skills. He was right. We can teach skills, but it is a lot more difficult to mold someone who is not a good cultural fit.

Our company sales strategy involved using the team approach, so the ability to effectively work with others was paramount. If someone had a core value of working independently, this would not have fit well in our culture. We needed people with high commitment levels who were willing to work hard to support others. Team success came first, so we wanted to make sure people joining the organization understood that. We needed people who communicated well and were driven to help their team succeed.

In Clayton Christianson's book *How Will You Measure Your Life* he wrote:

> "We hear a lot of stories about so called successful people, only to find out their professional success came at a huge cost to other areas of their lives. For many of us, one of the easiest mistakes to make is to focus on trying to over-satisfy the tangible trappings of professional success in the mistaken belief that those things will make us happy. Better salaries. A more prestigious title. A nicer office. They are, after all, what our friends and family see as signs we have "made it" professionally. [9]"

By understanding what matters most to us, we can plan accordingly to make sure we are going after our own personal definition of success.

Here are my examples of core values:

Commitment has always been important to me. First, commitment to my family is paramount, and I am grateful for my wife, children, and grandchildren. Family defines a large part of my mission in life. Commitment was also key on the sports and business teams I belonged to.

Trust is mandatory. With trust we can do anything. We know we will always be there for each other. Having a relationship built on trust is so powerful. Without trust we really do not have a foundation to work from. Trust for me is the value that everything is built on.

Respect is required. It does not matter what someone's status or job is; everyone deserves equal respect with no exceptions. Respect in the workplace should always be evident for everyone in the organization. Treating people with dignity and honoring their personal freedom are the right things to do.

Remember, your sales career is a *marathon*, not a sprint. By aligning your actions with your core values and goals, you will build a solid foundation for sustained, long-term success.

Take some time to reflect on what truly drives you. What motivates you to get out of bed in the morning? What are your passions and aspirations? Your answers will provide valuable insights into your career path and help align your sales efforts with your personal values.

My three core values are:

1. _____

2. _____

3. _____

Now let's explore the ten key principles of sales success.

The Sales Separators

TEN PRINCIPLES OF SUCCESS

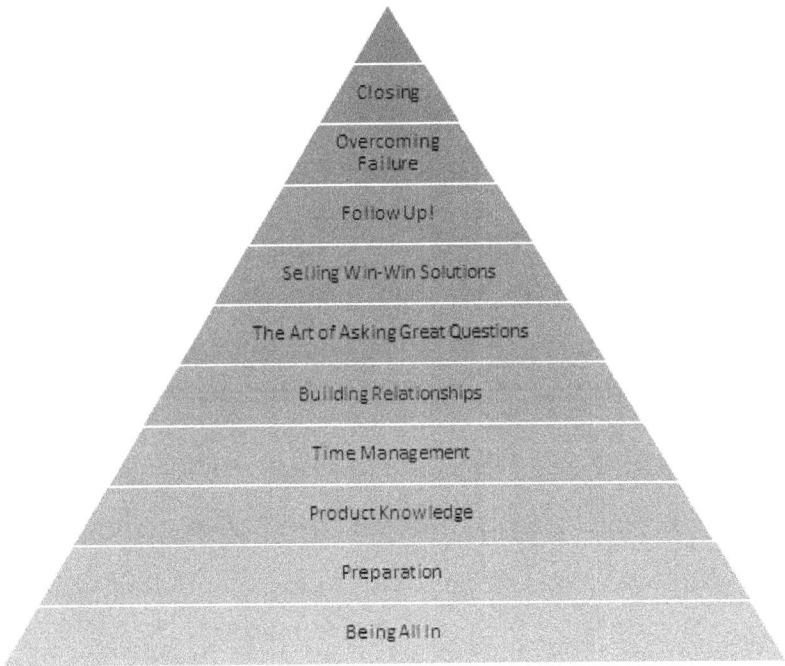

Closing

Overcoming Failure

Follow Up!

Selling Win-Win Solutions

The Art of Asking Great Questions

Building Relationships

Time Management

Product Knowledge

Preparation

Being All In

Sales Separator #1—Being All In

There is a difference between being interested and commitment. When you are interested in something, you do it only when it's convenient. When you're committed to something, you don't accept excuses, only results.

—Ken Blanchard

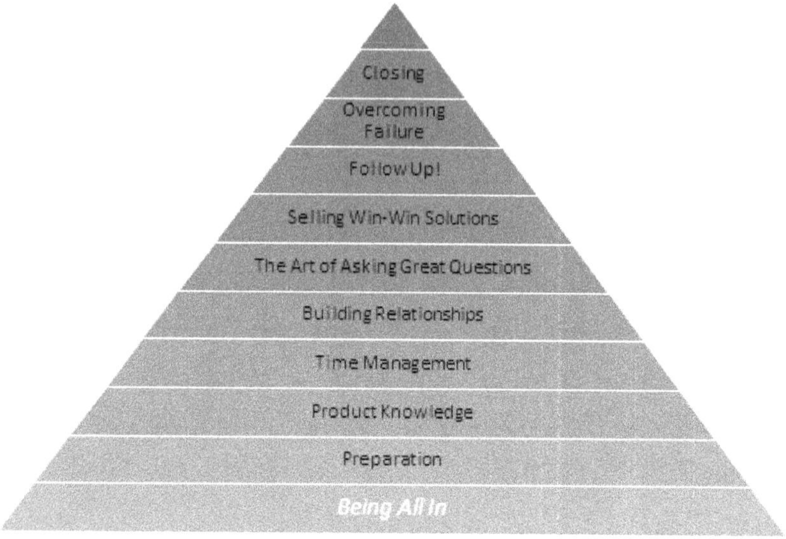
Closing
Overcoming Failure
Follow Up!
Selling Win-Win Solutions
The Art of Asking Great Questions
Building Relationships
Time Management
Product Knowledge
Preparation
Being All In

IT TAKES COMMITMENT

Success in sales hinges on unwavering, long-term dedication. It is about going beyond the basics, consistently surpassing expectations, and pouring your heart and energy into your work. When you are deeply committed, you will do whatever it takes to achieve your goals.

On my teams, I always sought individuals who brought more to their jobs than what was required. It is not just about fulfilling your job; it is about bringing that extra to it. I have collaborated with people who not only solved the immediate problem we were facing but also went a step further and introduced new, innovative ideas that pushed our business forward. This is the extra effort that sets you apart. People who consistently overdeliver are recognized as top performers, gain more opportunities with customers, and earn career promotions. Businesses seek individuals who do more than just show up; they need dedicated, trusted problem-solvers who can elevate their business.

As Seth Godin writes in *Linchpin*, "The only way to get what you're worth is to stand out, to exert emotional labor, to be seen as indispensable, and to produce interactions that organizations and people care deeply about."[10] When you are all in, you stand out in your organization.

Early in my career, my wife and I made a pivotal decision that shaped my professional path. Living in New Hampshire, I was traveling to customers in Maine weekly, requiring extensive overnight travel. I was away four nights a week, staying in hotels. Because we were starting a family, we did not see this as sustainable. My customers were huge paper mills in the corners of northern Maine. We decided to fold our tent and move to Bangor, Maine. This was a place where we had no family or friends but where I could better serve my customers. Bangor was central to my territory and allowed great access to key accounts. Despite the challenges, including eighteen inches of snow on Thanksgiving the first year, we were determined to provide exceptional service and get closer to customers.

The move paid off. Being geographically closer to my customers enabled me to increase my sales substantially and led to my territory being recognized a few years later as a top-performing area for the company. Customers appreciated the responsiveness and dedication, which led to closer relationships and increased sales. Plus, I got to spend more time with our two young daughters. Both our children were born in Bangor, and we cherish the memories and connections we made there. This experience taught me the true essence of being fully committed. It is about going beyond what is expected and making sacrifices to achieve your goals. This was not our only significant move; we later relocated to Charleston, South Carolina, to work from the company's home office, which also proved vital for my career.

Many of my customers had extremely high levels of commitment, and they had the same expectations of their suppliers. I remember speaking with one of my key customers after he had worked several weeks in a row with no time off to make sure a major investment in his operation was managed properly and on time. He was responsible for a huge manufacturing operation and a large staff of people. I asked him how he was doing after working long hours for several straight weeks. He said, "Tim, when you become a leader, you give up the right to complain." He set a strong example for his team because he was fully committed. He also conducted business with people who had the same dedication.

One Thanksgiving early in my career, we had plans to visit family in New Jersey. My parents had purchased tickets for the entire family to attend a Broadway show over the weekend. We were excited for the long weekend. The day before the holiday, as we were preparing to leave for the long drive to New Jersey from Maine, I received a call from a major customer. They informed me that I was getting an opportunity to get back the business that had gone to a competitor based on product performance. We supplied a specialty material used in the production of paper and our customers were huge paper mill operations. The paper mills are twenty-four seven operations and have high expectations of their suppliers. Having lost the business at this major account, I was under a lot of pressure to win it back. Getting the opportunity was great news. The other news was that they were going to start using my product in the mill on Thanksgiving Day and expected me to be there at 4:30a.m. to offer my support. I knew my family would be disappointed, but I had no choice. We stayed in Maine, and I worked throughout the weekend. My wife was disheartened not to spend Thanksgiving with family but as usual, incredibly supportive.

The Monday after the holiday weekend, my customer was not satisfied that our product made enough difference to their operation and put the competitor back on their machines. This was tough news to hear after canceling our Thanksgiving plans. I was not successful, but it was not because of a lack of effort. I did gain additional opportunities with this customer and eventually earned the business back. We were all in, and I would do it the same way all over again.

Having the goal of being a top sales performer involves placing your career as a big priority in your life. This can involve making difficult choices about your time. It is vital for you to embrace the fact that if you want to be very successful in your sales career, it will require full commitment.

Being all in means you are emotionally invested in supporting your customers and your company on a consistent basis.

STAY ENERGIZED

Being all in is necessary, but we need the energy to sustain it for the long run. It is challenging to maintain high levels of commitment long term. All top sales performers need to avoid burnout. This can happen if you are putting forth high amounts of effort without taking necessary breaks. Even the most committed people can lose their enthusiasm if they do not take the time to reenergize. This is critical because if you are not enthusiastic about serving your customers, your performance will suffer. I have seen very talented salespeople lose effectiveness later in their careers because they had not renewed their energy on a regular basis.

Take vacations each year to stay fresh. As in any long-term endeavor, breaks are mandatory. I remember running a twenty-six-mile marathon decades ago and the advice an experienced runner gave me. He said, "Don't miss any water stops even if you feel you don't need them. If you don't take the consistent breaks, you will pay the price at the end of the race." I was thankful for the advice and started hydrating the first mile. We all need a plan to recharge.

Here are some tips for keeping energy levels high:

- Take care of yourself: Go for walks, pursue hobbies, eat healthy, exercise, get rest.

- Take regular breaks: Plan your vacation time, step away, and recharge.

- Have goals outside work that you are passionate about. This could be running, education, or developing a new skill.

By taking care of yourself, you will maintain the energy necessary for long-term success.

KEY TAKEAWAYS

1. Success requires commitment.

2. Bring that extra effort and overdeliver.

3. Recharge and keep the energy level high.

Rate yourself 1–10 on being fully committed:

_____

What is holding you back?

_____

_____

_____

_____

_____

_____

_____

_____

_____

Sales Separator #2—Preparation

*Luck is What Happens When Preparation
Meets Opportunity.*

—Seneca

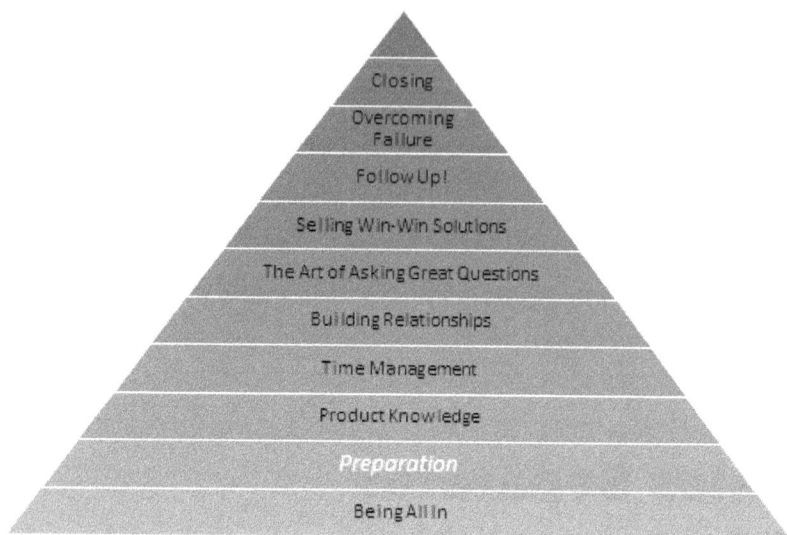

```
                    Closing
                  Overcoming
                    Failure
                  Follow Up!
              Selling Win-Win Solutions
          The Art of Asking Great Questions
              Building Relationships
                Time Management
               Product Knowledge
                   Preparation
                   Being All In
```

There is good reason boot camp, preseason, warm-up games, graduate programs, or any great training exists. It is to get people prepared! Competing and winning begin with preparation. Witness any great professional at work and be assured they have spent incredible amounts of time training to be the best.

Preparation is all the background work that has gone into the moment when the professional delivers in a crucial situation. Selling is no different. The best salespeople excel in this area. They review notes from previous calls, check on deliveries, prepare questions, deliver proposals, and always stay one step ahead. Top sales professionals take the time to plan, confirm appointments, and manage key follow-ups. Preparation is crucial for everyone in sales. It includes a thorough understanding of your industry, the company you work for, and your territory. Great sales profession-als are experts in mastering detail. Customers appreciate well-prepared salespeople as it shows respect for their time and gives them the confidence to do business with them. Being properly prepared gives you the confidence to pursue your goals.

WHAT BUSINESS ARE YOU IN? STUDY AND GET INVOLVED IN YOUR INDUSTRY

Part of your professional preparation is having a solid understanding of the industry you work in. Whether you are in software, manufacturing, or finance, take the time to study your market. Utilize resources such as websites, trade organizations, and your network to learn as much as you can. Stay informed about how your industry is doing and what the trends are. Sign up for courses that focus on the business you work in. If your customers are public, read their quarterly earnings reports. These are helpful to track how a customer is doing financially, areas of concern in their business, and how they perceive the business outlook. Keep asking questions about the industry you work in so you can learn as much as possible. Get involved in trade groups and attend conferences so you gain knowledge and expand your network. The more you know, the more effective you will be.

Here are some examples of what you need to know:

- The market you serve: How big is it, and what is the growth rate?

- Market leaders: Which companies lead and why?

- The competition: Who are your top competitors?

- Industry trends: What is affecting your industry long term?

WHO DO YOU WORK FOR? LEARN ABOUT YOUR COMPANY

Being knowledgeable about your company builds credibility and trust with customers. Having in-depth knowledge about your organization helps you articulate its mission and address customer questions effectively. Customers respect salespeople who know their firms well. You need to be able to explain the key attributes of the organization you work for. Be highly interested in where you work, so you can communicate why customers should do business with you. You represent your company, and customers will expect you to educate them on the important facets of your organization. Be prepared to update your customers about the place you work.

We would start most sales presentations with a few comments about our company. A concise explanation will help your prospects get to know about the culture and key facts relative to your organization. What makes you unique in the market you serve?

Recommendations to gain in-depth company knowledge include:

- Utilize your company resources: Websites, financial reports, training courses, and internal communications.

- Attend internal update meetings and take note of major significant changes.

- Seek out internal expertise: Network with colleagues across different departments.

- Ask questions: Seek information from management or subject matter experts.

- Keep learning: Stay updated on company news, product launches, and any important internal changes.

Here are a few examples of what you need to know:

- Your corporate culture and core values.

- Your company's revenue.

- Where the products are produced.

- The markets your company serves.

- The company's strategy for the products you sell.

HOW ABOUT YOUR TERRITORY?

A thorough understanding of your sales territory is essential for effective strategic sales planning. By analyzing your business, you can identify opportunities, prioritize efforts, and develop targeted strategies. Your territory is your own business, so you need to know everything about it. Since this is the field that you play on, make sure you take the time to study it carefully.

Ideas to become knowledgeable about your territory:

- Assess its total market potential.

- Determine your market share and key competitors.

- Identify key accounts and top potential customers and develop strategies for each.

- Leverage technology: Use customer relationship software and sales analytics tools to optimize territory management.

- Understand which customers are industry leaders and why.

FIND GREAT MENTORS

In the book *Mastery* by George Leonard, one of the key points is the importance of getting great instruction on anything we want to learn. Excellence will not just happen; we need the wisdom and guidance of mentors. Great teachers can be tremendous resources throughout your career. In your sales journey, you will need to learn from others to continue to improve and grow. Finding mentors both inside and outside your company will be key to your preparation and development. I had great mentors who were managers and company leaders as well as customers who all had a major impact on my development. They helped me grow in so many ways as a leader, salesperson, and manager. Developing strong mentor relationships inside and outside your organization will pay big dividends for you.

Early in my career, one of my mentors recommended I go back to school for a master's degree in business. Based on his encouragement, I pursued a local master's program, which turned out to be a great learning experience. It was a lot of work, but I am grateful for the excellent instructors and education I received. I applied many of the lessons from the program throughout my career.

A key customer of mine influenced me to improve my analytical and computer skills. He even arranged for me to work with one of their best Six Sigma resources, which proved to be incredibly beneficial. Many companies adopted the Six Sigma approach to statistical process improvement to reduce waste and variability in their operations. Training in this area was vital, and I used these skills regularly in my sales and management positions.

I also had the privilege of traveling extensively with two outstanding technical experts in my industry and learned a great deal from both. Learning from them helped me improve my technical expertise and establish better credibility with my customers. I would travel with each of them on occasion and bring them to my major accounts. Their credibility was so high in my industry that all my main contacts would take the time to meet with them no matter how busy they were. It was a privilege to learn from amazing people who helped me grow.

In the company I worked for, we created a sales mentor program in which recent sales hires are assigned to work with some of our most experienced salespeople. Mentors and mentees work together for six months and are provided with a curriculum of sales best practices that we developed internally. The goal of the program is to provide sales training in a real setting, where our new hires can watch, participate with, and learn from our experienced sales pros. The program has worked very well, and many of our new hires have become mentors in the program. It is also a terrific way to recognize many of our sales pros by having them in a teaching role. It is great to see the impact that mentors have had teaching people who are new to the organization.

With the adoption of work from home policies at companies, it can be challenging to create mentoring opportunities. Because there may be less office interaction today than historically, using technology to interface with mentors can be a great option. I have experienced working virtually as a mentor with an executive, and this has proven to be effective. Making sure there is a weekly virtual meeting recurring in our calendars has been very helpful. Using technology to expand your reach can open new opportunities for mentoring relationships.

Tips for cultivating strong mentor relationships:

- Identify and reach out to potential mentors with experience you admire. You will be surprised how many people want to help you.

- Ask for help, guidance, and wisdom from experienced professionals.

- Use technology to communicate often with your mentors.

- Listen to, learn, and apply the best practices your mentors teach you.

Looking over the horizon in your industry, what skills will you need in the future? These could be presentation skills, an understanding of artificial intelligence, or something else. Be prepared for any changes that may come your way. Preparation is where success starts. It takes time and effort, but practicing great preparation consistently will provide you with fewer surprises and more opportunities.

Recommendations on preparation:

- Use a process to prepare and always be one step ahead.

- Visualize what you need to accomplish first and then backfill the details. Your imagination is a powerful tool; use it. Constantly ask, "What if?"

- Arrive early, have questions prepared, and confirm your appointments.

- Give yourself more time than you think you need. This can mean starting a project early, preparing a presentation, or traveling to a customer. Always function as if there will be an obstacle that could delay you.

Always have contingency plans. If the presentation technology fails in a customer meeting, can you deliver the material without slides?

KEY TAKEAWAYS

1. Study your industry, company, and territory.

2. Use a system for preparation.

3. Find and cultivate mentor relationships.

Rate yourself 1–10 on preparation:

_____

These are the three things I will do to improve my preparation:

1._____

2._____

3._____

Everyone needs a system for being prepared. Here is an example of a weekly planning sheet that may be helpful.

Weekly Planning and Preparation Sheet

Date:

1._____

2._____

3._____

Top three goals for the next ninety days

1._____

2._____

3._____

People to contact this week

1._____

2._____

3._____

4._____

Key follow-ups from last week

1._____

2._____

3._____

Action items for this week

1._____

2._____

3._____

4._____

5._____

Sales Separator #3—Product Knowledge

If you can't explain it simply, you don't understand it well enough.

—Albert Einstein

BECOME A PRODUCT EXPERT

Don't you prefer dealing with a salesperson who has expertise about the products they are selling? A knowledgeable salesperson builds confidence in the customer's decision-making process. Having a thorough grasp of the products you sell is key to establishing credibility and trust with your customers. By becoming an expert, you can effectively communicate the benefits and value your products provide. As Neil Rackham states in his book *Major Account Sales Strategy*, "Understanding the range of problems your products can solve is the first step toward setting effective sales call objectives . . ."[11] It is essential to learn the story behind how your products can provide value to customers.

As Seth Godin writes in *This Is Marketing*, "Our calling is to make a difference. A chance to make things better for those we seek to serve"[12] Your product needs to tell a story that resonates with customers. Reflect on your own significant purchases and the people you interacted with. Wasn't the experience better when the person was an expert? Investing time in learning about your products will help you build a competitive advantage. A product expert can guide a customer smoothly through the buying process and answer questions, helping close sales.

My experience with some salespeople is that product expertise is viewed as something a specialist in their organization has and can support them when needed with customers. The belief is that a great relationship with a customer will carry the day in closing a sale. While great relationships are essential, all salespeople will be tested on their knowledge of the products they sell. People will have more confidence making major purchases from you if they perceive you as an expert in what you are selling. I always believed if you are selling a product, you need to be prepared to answer every possible question someone may ask.

The best sales pros I worked with could teach a class on the products they sold. They learned about their products so thoroughly that their customers considered them subject matter experts and consultants to their business. The best make sure they develop the knowledge needed to convey their product offerings' value to help solve their customers' challenges. Study and understand your products so thoroughly that you become a resource for your customers. It will take time, but it will be worth the effort.

Very early in my career, I traveled to the home office of the company I worked for to attend product training. When I arrived, the manager responsible for all United States sales said he wanted to have lunch with me that Friday before I headed home to see how the training went. I knew the lunch would be a test, and he would quiz me on what I learned that week. I prepared for that lunch as if it were an exam. As I was new in my sales role, my product knowledge was not strong, but I was determined to pass the lunch test. My trainer did a great job teaching me, and we spent a lot of time that week reviewing our product offerings.

Friday came, and as we were about to begin our debriefing lunch in the company cafeteria, the manager said to me, "Okay, Tim, tell me about our products." I was prepared and launched into a summary of the products we sold and how they were applied. He was surprised that I was able to describe many of our key products and applications. My boss at the time was also there, and afterward, we critiqued how I did. It was very satisfying to know that being prepared made a huge difference. This experience enhanced my product knowledge as I had no choice but to learn quickly. That week of training was a great start to establishing product expertise I could share with customers and enhance my sales effectiveness.

USE TECHNICAL RESOURCES WITHIN YOUR COMPANY

There will be sales situations that require additional technical product expertise to support your sales efforts. On many occasions, I had outstanding technical support, and customers appreciated hearing from experts at the appropriate time in the sales cycle. When you have people traveling with you to customers, take the time to prepare and rehearse thoroughly before your meeting. Your customer visits will be more effective with proper preparation. Bringing in the right technical resource to speak with your customers occasionally can be a differentiator for you in winning business. You can also learn more about the products and applications you are selling when spending time with technical experts.

Strategies for enhancing product knowledge:

- Attend product training and make it a priority: Participate in all available training sessions and workshops.

- Be able to articulate the key features, benefits, and value story of the products you are selling.

- Seek out experts: Connect and spend time with colleagues who have deep product knowledge.

- Practice presenting your products to build confidence and improve delivery.

- Stay updated: Keep informed about product updates, new features, and industry trends.

By investing time in product knowledge, you will become a trusted adviser to your customers, and you will have a competitive edge in your territory.

YOUR ELEVATOR PITCH

Everyone is busy, and you may find there are times when your customers have just a few minutes to see you. In these situations, you need to provide a quick, compelling explanation about yourself, your company, and the products you are selling. An elevator pitch is a concise and memorable message that makes a strong impression and captures attention. Delivering a well-prepared elevator pitch will also boost your confidence when dealing with customers. I even made it a practice when interviewing potential sales candidates to provide an elevator speech about themselves.

Being able to concisely articulate the features and benefits of the products you sell will prove helpful in your communication with customers. Preparing your pitch on the products you sell helps you ascertain the key highlights of what you are selling. Preparing this way will help you condense the product attributes down to what is essential for people to know.

One time I was visiting a key customer and decision-maker for the first time with one of our account representatives. I had just taken over the managerial role in a large region of the country and was visiting accounts. After we shook hands, the customer sat back in his chair, looked at my business card, and asked, "So, Tim, what's your claim to fame?" Never saw that question coming! It was such a direct way of having me give an elevator speech about myself. I handled it fairly well, but I never forgot that experience and made sure I was ready in the future for questions like that.

Basic structure for your elevator pitch:

- Who you are: Briefly introduce yourself and your company.

- What you do: Clearly explain your company's core business and value proposition.

- Who you can help: Identify your target customer or market.

- Call to action: Encourage the listener to take the next step, such as scheduling a meeting or requesting more information.

Practice your elevator pitch until you can deliver it naturally and confidently. Remember, the goal is to create interest and curiosity, not to overwhelm your listener with information.

KEY TAKEAWAYS

1. Have deep knowledge of the products you are selling.

2. Create a product training plan.

3. Prepare your elevator pitch about yourself, products you sell, and your company.

Rate yourself 1–10 on product knowledge:

_____

What is your elevator pitch about your company (history, culture, markets served)?

_____

_____

_____

_____

_____

_____

My improvement plan to increase my product knowledge includes:

1._____

2._____

3._____

Sales Separator #4—Time Management

Lack of direction, not lack of time is the problem. We all have 24-hour days.

—Zig Ziglar

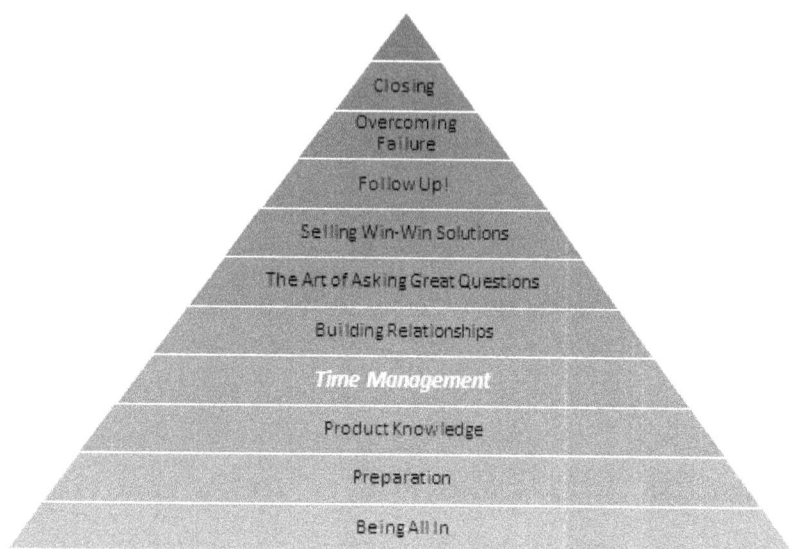

Time is our most precious resource. As Oliver Burkeman wrote in *Four Thousand Weeks: Time Management for Mortals*, "It follows that time management broadly defined, should be everyone's chief concern. Arguably, time management is all life is."[13] We are as good as where we spend our time.

In sales, you are in the time management business. Effective time management is crucial for maximizing your productivity and effectiveness. Each day you waste is a day you can never get back. With only a limited amount of time to make an impact, it is vital to focus on the right tasks and customers. You cannot solve everyone's problems, so you must decide which customers to prioritize and how much time to allocate to them.

You'll serve many people. You'll profit from a few.

—*Seth Godin*

In the book *The 80/20 Principle*, Richard Koch writes, "The 80/20 Principle asserts that a minority of causes, inputs, or effort usually lead to a majority of the results, outputs, or rewards. Taken literally, this means that, for example, 80 percent of what you achieve in your job comes from 20 percent of the time spent."[14] In sales, most revenue and profit will come from a select group of customers. Understanding this is crucial. Build a strategic plan that targets the right accounts and allocates your time effectively. Without this focus, even the most talented salesperson can struggle to achieve success.

To manage your time well, you need to have a thorough understanding of your territory and the market you work in. Historical and potential sales data will help guide you. With experience, you will gain a deeper understanding of your territory and become more effective at planning your schedule. It is essential to measure and document your time to make necessary adjustments. It is not uncommon to overweight your attention to some customers. Documenting your customer visits will help make sure you are allocating your time most effectively.

Early in my career, one of my customers required a significant amount of my attention. We had several projects underway with them, and this involved tremendous resources and focus. My time was overweighted toward this account for quite a while, and I knew my other customers deserved more attention. As I became aware of this, I began to reach out to my other large accounts and thought I had done well communicating with them.

Apparently, I had not. When I visited one of my key accounts, they told me they had decided to try another supplier. I knew this customer had not received enough of my time, and I felt like I had been blindsided by the competition. The truth was if I had paid enough attention to them, I would have had a solid chance to keep the competition away. This was a painful lesson in time management and the fact that my schedule needed to be managed more carefully.

If you think you are not paying enough attention to an account, do not hesitate. Reach out and contact them to make sure they know how important their relationship is. Do not fall behind on your customer communication and invite the competition to take your business.

On my sales teams, we allocated resources based on key factors such as account potential, our position within the account, the competitive landscape, and where the customer was in the buying cycle. We regularly reviewed and adjusted our strategies as circumstances changed. By targeting our efforts where we could be most successful, we maximized our effectiveness.

Here are some tips for effective time management:

- Apply the 80/20 principle to planning your schedule.

- Prioritize your accounts by sales revenue, potential, and profitability.

- Use Outlook to manage and prioritize email.

- Become proficient with CRM tools within your organization.

- Create a sales call frequency plan based on territory metrics.

- Make a daily plan on how you will spend your time.

- Allocate specific time blocks for different activities, such as sales calls, prospecting, and administrative tasks.

- Eliminate activities that are not providing value to you.

OWN YOUR MONDAY

Either you run the day or the day runs you.

—Jim Rohn

Many people dread Mondays, but it does not have to be that way. When I was in field sales, I found Mondays exciting. Starting the week with a well-structured plan sets a positive direction to accomplish your goals. If you do not have a plan in place, you will scramble to catch up, and the rest of the week may suffer. By owning your Monday, you can ensure a productive start to your week. Start planning your Monday the week before so you can hit the ground running after the weekend. When you have a plan, you feel more confident and are more effective.

MANAGE YOUR CALENDAR

To be effective at managing your time, you need to take control of your calendar. Plan at least two weeks ahead, and while you can schedule further out, two weeks is a manageable period. Use an electronic calendar to stay disciplined and audit your time regularly. Whatever system you use, it is vital to keep it updated so you are never late, never miss an appointment, and keep your commitments.

CONDUCT A TIME ASSESSMENT EXERCISE

In Peter Drucker's book *The Effective Executive*, he states that "recording time, managing time, and consolidating time is the foundation of executive effectiveness."[14] When I read that, it gave me the motivation to do a time assessment. When I started my last management role, I would be driving home from the office asking myself, *What did I accomplish today?* I found my time became consumed by so many different meetings, emails, presentations, and interviews it was difficult to feel a sense of accomplishment.

By conducting a time assessment exercise, I discovered areas where my time was overly consumed and areas that needed more focus. This ongoing process helped me allocate my time more effectively. I could see patterns in how my time was spent. This was helpful in my becoming more focused and effective. I could see that planning and budget meetings started in early summer and ran into the fall. This required a lot of analyzing information and putting internal presentations together. I learned that the first two quarters of the year were much better times for me to travel to see customers. The time assessment made me more aware of periods in the year that were committed internally so I could plan accordingly.

How you spend your time is so important and conducting a time assessment will provide helpful insight. Review your calendar for the past six months and categorize your time into buckets like office time, customer visits, meetings, and travel. Assess whether you are spending time with the most important customers and if you need to adjust.

Examples of time assessment categories:

- Customer visits

- Office time

- Meetings

- Travel

- Training

- Administrative tasks

By understanding where your time goes, you can ensure it is spent in the right areas to make you more effective.

KEY TAKEAWAYS

1. Time is your most precious resource. Manage it carefully.

2. Own your Monday and manage your calendar.

3. Use the 80/20 principle for effective time management.

4. Conduct a time assessment exercise.

Rate yourself 1–10 on time management:

_____

These are the three things I can do to improve my time management:

1._____

2._____

3._____

Sales Separator #5—Building Relationships

You can make more friends in two months being interested in other people than you can in two years trying to get other people interested in you.

—Dale Carnegie

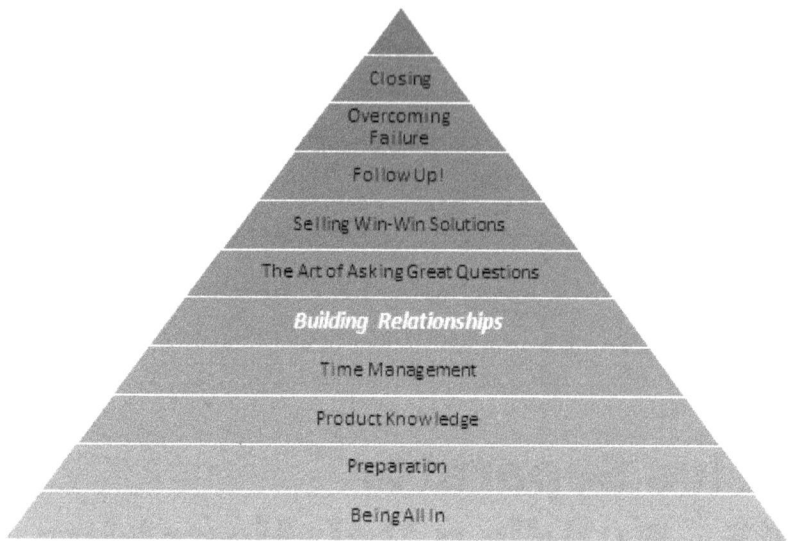

Building relationships is critical to success, both personally and professionally. Your ability to connect with others is the foundation of your career and business achievements. Key relationships, inside and outside your organization, will shape your future opportunities. Investing time and effort in building these relationships is essential for any professional. A mentor once advised me to always surround myself with good people, and it has proven to be invaluable advice.

Strong relationships are the cornerstone of sales success. Trust and rapport with customers lead to long-term partnerships and increased sales. Customers enjoy doing business with people who are authentic. As Seth Godin wrote in the book *Linchpin*, "The individual in the organization who collects, connects, and nurtures relationships is indispensable. This isn't about recording the information in a database somewhere. This is about holding the relationships as sacred as they deserve to be."[15] Spending the time to develop lasting relationships is critical.

ENGAGE PEOPLE TO SHARE THEIR STORIES

Everyone has a story to tell, and it is our job to ask the right questions to let them share it. I have been amazed by the stories I have heard over the years. I am always curious about people's backgrounds and interests. When interviewing people, I like to ask candidates to tell me a tale about themselves that defines who they truly are. This question often surprises people, and it has been incredible to hear amazing stories from people. The comeback where a person had to dig deep to achieve what they were going after is always impressive.

Looking back, one conversation stands out. I was interviewing a candidate for a sales position who had excellent technical qualifications but no sales experience. He had outstanding industry experience, but I wanted to know more about what truly motivated him. When I asked him to tell a story about himself, there was a very long pause—so long I did not think he would answer the question. Just as I thought the interview would end without hearing his answer, he leaned over the table and looked me in the eyes. He said, "Mr. Gallagher, I'm not much of a storyteller, but I'm the hardest-working God-fearing family man you have ever met." I could see his determination to succeed! We hired him and he proved himself to be a highly motivated and outstanding sales representative who brought excellent value to our customers.

Personal relationships are essential in every area of life, and they require time and commitment. Without key connections with customers and colleagues, my career would have turned out very differently. Strong bonds with people foster more opportunities and better collaboration, improving both sales performance and career progression. Showing genuine interest in other people is essential. While skills will help start your career, it will be the relationships you build that will ultimately make you successful.

BUILDING RAPPORT

Building rapport involves finding common interests with people. Discover what someone is interested in and encourage them to talk about it. People enjoy discussing what they are passionate about, and it is gratifying to have someone genuinely interested in what they are saying. To be a skilled conversationalist, you must be able to speak on a wide variety of topics. You do not need expertise—just a few bits of information so you can converse with different people who have wide interests. Reading the *Wall Street Journal*, *New York Times*, or local paper is a terrific way to stay abreast of news, events, and trends. I like to ask what people are reading. It gives me insight into what they are interested in, and many times provides informative book ideas to pursue. Being well read will help you be a more effective conversationalist. Building rapport is an important skill, and the key is to be interested in what the other person is enthusiastic about.

KEEPING RELATIONSHIPS ABOVE NEUTRAL

When people first meet, they start their relationship in a neutral state as they are getting acquainted. From here, the relationship can go in two directions. They can connect and build a solid relationship, even becoming friends. It is true in business that people buy from those they like. A positive relationship is one that remains above neutral. We should always strive to take our relationships above neutral and maintain them there. Positive connections with people foster greater business relationships.

Conversely, a relationship can drop below neutral if one party acts dishonestly or against the other's best interests. *Once below, it is exceedingly difficult to bring a relationship back to neutral.* In business, things do not always go as planned. Shipments can be late, quality might decline, and prices may change. Salespeople often manage these sensitive issues, and it is crucial to maintain at least a neutral relationship with customers. Arrogance, failing to follow up, and acting self-interested can harm relationships. Always work to keep your relationships above neutral.

My customers were under significant pressure to perform in their manufacturing operations, and occasionally they would need to vent. Sometimes I was the recipient of this. The best thing I could do was not to be defensive. This would not have gotten me anywhere or helped the relationship. Remaining calm and quiet kept our relationship above neutral. They had the space to express themselves and did not feel they had to defend their position. Many times, I would see them a day or two later once they'd had a chance to reflect, and we would be right back to our solid relationship. People are under a lot of stress sometimes, and we need to empathize and put ourselves in their shoes. There may be times in your career when your customers may be frustrated and need to express themselves. Choose your response wisely and do not think short term by being defensive.

Always keep your relationships at least neutral. Once below neutral, it is very difficult to recover.

Relationships are reciprocal. Helping someone often leads to a returned favor. Small tokens of appreciation, like a card or lunch invitation, are a great way to check in. One of my mentors was outstanding at building relationships. Aside from having great people skills, he was the first to call when colleagues were promoted or send flowers when they needed support. He made sure people knew he cared about them.

THE LITTLE THINGS MEAN EVERYTHING

My career depended on key relationships with people who worked in manufacturing environments. Many of my contacts worked long shifts, so anything I could do to help them have a better work experience was appreciated. I would routinely bring in treats like pastries such as strudel, muffins, or even pies to brighten their day. Everyone was very appreciative, and there were many times I needed the support of folks who ran the manufacturing operations.

One time we were upgrading our product offering in a key account, and it was not going according to plan. It was my idea to upgrade to a new product design, and we had spent the day attempting to implement it. I believed that the upgraded design would bring more value to this customer, and they gave me the opportunity to showcase it. As much as we tried, the new product was not improving the customer's operation. I left late that afternoon when there was a shift change, thinking we would go back to our previous product early the next day. My key decision-maker was extremely disappointed, as we all were.

As I was driving down the highway, an idea came to me that we had not tried but I believed would work. I called the lead operator at the customer site who had just started his shift. He and I had worked together on his machine previously. I asked him if I came back to the site, would he collaborate with me on second shift, implementing the idea I was proposing? He agreed, and together we worked that evening and were successful in getting the new product design to work. Without his help, this would never have happened. The next day, the manager of the operation was satisfied that the new product was providing additional value and now became the standard.

This is just one example of the tremendous people I worked with and how important every relationship is. Everyone in your accounts is important, and you never know when you will need someone's help.

RECOGNITION IS KEY

People love to be recognized! Be the person who recognizes and gives credit to others. Recognition boosts morale, fosters loyalty, and strengthens relationships. Appreciating someone's efforts can make their day. As Mark Twain said, "I can live on a good compliment two weeks with nothing else to eat."[16] Look for opportunities to recognize the people you work with. Not only are you giving them the recognition they deserve, but you are also displaying the value you place on the magnificent work people do. Prioritizing recognition creates a culture where employees feel valued and motivated.

Effective recognition includes:

- Being specific: Clearly mention the behavior or achievement you are recognizing.

- Being timely: Recognize promptly to maximize the impact.

- Being sincere: Show genuine appreciation.

- Public recognition: Celebrate achievements publicly to inspire others.

MAKE OTHERS THE HERO

In Peter Drucker's book *The Effective Executive*, he writes, "Don't think or say 'I,' think and say 'we.'"[17] One of the best things you can be known for in your career is attributing success to others. Even if you played a crucial role in a win, stay humble and give credit to others. Self-promotion rarely goes over well. A great manager once told me that promotions come from being pushed up by colleagues, not pulled up by leadership. Humility is essential and will help your career significantly. Be known as the person who makes others feel like winners. Make your customers winners by helping them improve their business. When you have wins with customers, make sure you give them the credit. Growing existing business or obtaining new customers is all the recognition we need.

Strategies for strong relationships:

- Be genuinely interested in people.

- Stay in touch with regular communication.

- Build rapport with people.

- Be friendly to everyone you meet, no matter who they are.

- Be proactive in your relationships. Be the first to call or write.

YOUR TOP TEN CONTACTS

You can only maintain so many close contacts. In Malcolm Gladwell's book *The Tipping Point*, he points to research by Robin Dunbar that states that people can have five intimate friends, fifteen good friends, and about 150 acquaintances. Prioritize your key contacts by maintaining key details about them, such as birthdays and hobbies. Focus on key contacts within your customers' organizations. These are critical relationships for your business. Do the same within your own organization to advance your career. Look for shared interests and stay informed on current events to engage in relevant conversations. Your key customers and colleagues can only have so many close contacts. Make sure you are one of them.

KEY TAKEAWAYS

1. Cultivate relationships with customers, your company, and your industry.

2. Keep your relationships above neutral.

3. Recognize people and make others the hero.

Rate yourself 1–10 on building relationships:

_____

Here are three action items to improve my relationships:

1._____

2._____

3._____

My top ten business contacts (company and industry):

1._____

2._____

3._____

4._____

5._____

6._____

7. _____

8. _____

9. _____

10. _____

Sales Separator #6—The Art of Asking Great Questions

Successful people ask a lot more questions during sales calls than do their less successful colleagues. We found that these less successful people tend to do most of the talking.

—Neil Rackham

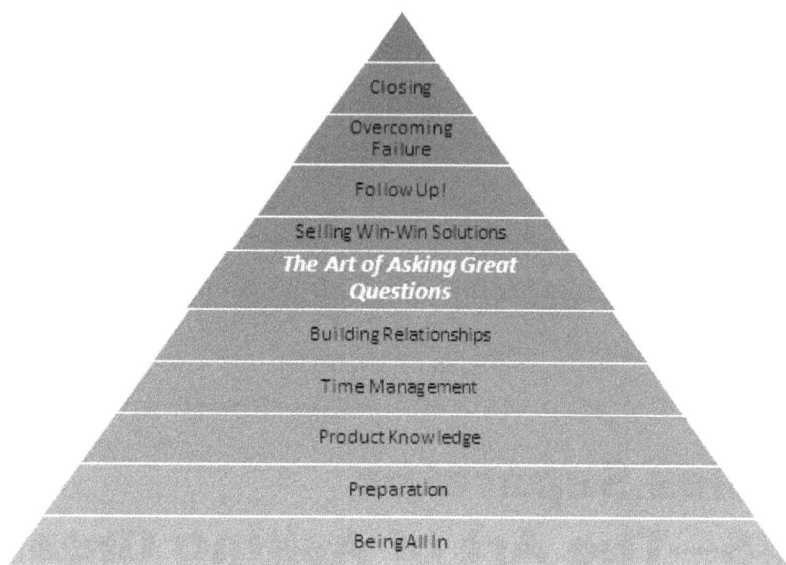

According to Sales Insights Lab, top-performing sales pros don't necessarily talk less, but they get their prospects talking more.

Understanding customer challenges hinges on how effective you are at asking great questions. Practicing and developing this skill are crucial. By making the right inquiries, you can identify customer needs, establish rapport, and effectively present your solutions.

It never ceases to amaze me how seldom I receive great questions, in either business or social settings. When was the last time someone asked you something insightful that made you really think? When someone asks me an interesting question, I thank them because I hear them so rarely. Mastering this skill allows us to understand people and the issues they face. Conversations thrive on a mutual exchange of information in which both parties benefit.

UNCOVERING THE GAP IN SATISFACTION

In the book *Major Account Sales Strategy,* Neil Rackham writes, "Our studies of success consistently demonstrated that the ability to uncover and develop dissatisfaction is the most important of all the selling skills."[18] To identify business opportunities, you must ask insightful, open-ended questions that engage customers. Your inquiry efforts need to be targeted to the areas where your products and solutions can add value. To do this effectively, you should have your questions prepared prior to the customer appointment.

Often you will hear customers say they are satisfied with the status quo. My experience is that everyone is unhappy about something. Every business can improve, and it is our job to engage the prospect to communicate their key issues. By asking the right questions, you can uncover areas in their business that need improvement and where you can add value.

Sample questions for uncovering the gap in satisfaction:

- I appreciate that you are currently having success this quarter. What aspect of your business could be improved to bring more value to the stakeholders?

- What would success look like if your business was operating at 100 percent?

Skilled conversationalists ask a lot of questions. Observe a successful salesperson, and you will find someone adept at getting people to talk.

Types of questions to consider:

- **Open-ended questions:** Encourage customers to share their thoughts and feelings about their business.

  Example: "What are the three biggest challenges you currently face in your business? How do you feel about your business performance?"

- **Probing questions:** Uncover underlying needs and motivations.

  Example: "What is the most critical area your business can improve on now?"

- **Clarifying questions:** To ensure understanding.

  Example: "To be clear, you mentioned that the biggest area we can help in is productivity; is that right?"

- **Summarizing questions:** Recap key points to confirm understanding.

  Example: "You mentioned that improving your operations productivity, reducing turnover, and hitting profitability targets were the priorities at this point; is that correct?"

Asking questions is not merely about gathering information; it is about forging genuine connections with your customers. By actively listening and responding thoughtfully, you can foster productive and positive conversations.

CHALLENGE YOURSELF TO ASK GREAT QUESTIONS

You can practice asking people questions whether in your personal or professional life. If you meet someone new, challenge yourself to find out what you can about them. Use social situations to become more adept at engaging people by leading great conversations.

When we skied in Maine as a family, the chair lift took about ten minutes to get from the base of the mountain to the top. On the lift, there were usually a few people I had never met. I would challenge myself to see how much information I could find out about each person in the limited amount of time we had. The first question I asked was where they lived, and then the conversation would build from there. It was fun, and I usually learned something interesting about the people we were with. My family did not always appreciate my questions as we went up the lift, but they knew I only had ten minutes before we started to ski down the mountain. It was a challenging and fun exercise to improve the way I asked questions and engaged with people.

The art of conversation lies in listening.

—*Malcolm Forbes*

THE IMPORTANCE OF LISTENING

Effective listening is essential to successful communication. While asking great questions is crucial, making the effort to understand people is even more important. I value doing business with someone who listens attentively. This skill helps us understand others so we can find solutions to their problems. We have all experienced someone asking us a question only to follow with another one before we have time to reply to the first. This leaves us feeling that we are not being listened to. It is important to let people feel heard and ensure we are not dominating the conversation.

Patience is key in conversations to allow information to flow naturally and make the other person comfortable. Listening is an essential skill for all of us to improve. Though we all like sharing our stories, our job is to encourage others to share theirs. Let conversations develop organically without rushing. Silence can be uncomfortable, but it is okay. Experience will teach you that quiet moments in conversations are normal.

Body language also plays a vital role in communication. Positive affirmations, whether verbal or nonverbal, can energize the conversation. People feel valued and respected when they have our full attention. Working on this skill will benefit you both professionally and personally.

No one ever lost a sale by listening effectively.

Tips for improving listening skills:

- Focus on the speaker: Maintain eye contact, avoid distractions, and show genuine interest.

- Be aware of how much you are talking versus listening.

- Ask clarifying questions: This will help demonstrate engagement and understanding.

- Summarize key points: Recap main ideas to confirm you have heard the key points in the conversation.

- Practice empathy: Understand the speaker's perspective by putting yourself in their shoes.

- Avoid interrupting: Allow the speaker to finish their thoughts before responding.

Listening is an active skill that demands practice and patience. By becoming a better listener, you will enhance your personal and professional relationships.

KEY TAKEAWAYS

1. Great questions help us understand people and the challenges they face.

2. Prepare questions to uncover the gap in satisfaction.

3. Work to develop listening skills.

Rate yourself 1–10 on asking great questions.

_____

Here are two ways I will improve my listening skills:

1._____

2._____

List two questions to uncover the customer's gap in satisfaction in your business:

1._____

_____

2._____

_____

Sales Separator #7—Selling Win-Win Solutions

In God we trust, all others must bring data.

—W. Edwards Deming

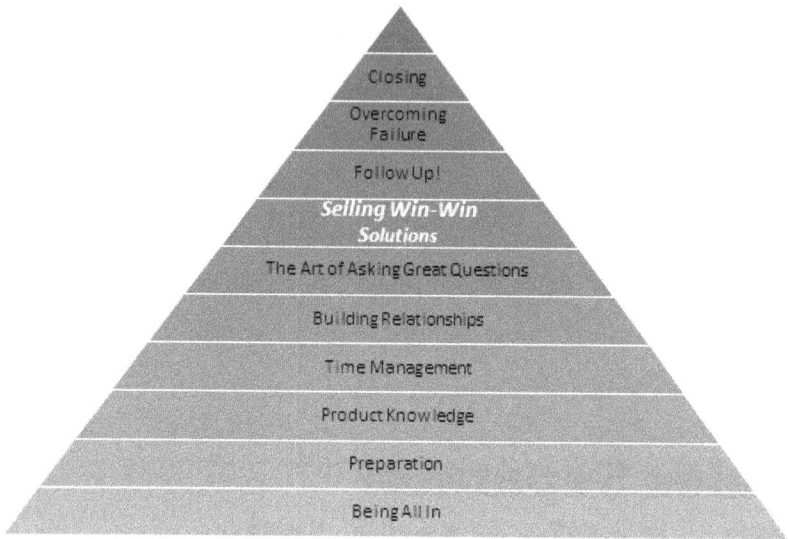

Articulating and documenting the total value of your products or services to customers are critical to closing sales. By clearly demonstrating how your products solve customer problems and deliver tangible benefits, you will build a compelling case for why people should do business with you. As the book *Major Account Sales Strategy* states, "Differentiation is how you convince the customer that you are different from the competition. . . . The objective of competitive differentiation is to make your product distinct in the customer's mind from other available alternatives."[19] You must articulate the financial benefits the customer will receive by using your products.

IT IS NOT JUST PRICE; TOTAL VALUE IS THE KEY

Understanding the value your products can bring to a customer's business is essential. The product you sell may initially cost more than the competition, but you are selling total value. The value story must provide a compelling case that your customer's business will improve by using the product you are selling. This can take different forms such as material cost savings, quality improvements, enhanced service, quicker delivery, better production performance for their operation, or other benefits. Communicating the business case can be the key differentiator in obtaining a major sale.

In my first sales position, I worked for a small business that sold maintenance products to schools and supermarket chains. The owner of the company had sold a large national supermarket chain on using our floor products in their stores. The account was huge, and we had a full-time representative visiting their stores to check in on our performance. The competition was constantly going after our business, and we were frequently asked by the customer's corporate purchasing people to prove our value by having product trials in one of their stores.

We would be assigned to take an aisle in one of their stores, and from one a.m. to five a.m., we had to remove the floor finish and put down three coats of fresh floor product. This had to be done when the store was closed, and our work had to be completed before the store reopened early in the morning. Each of our competitors was assigned the same exercise for comparison in other aisles in the store.

We were then required to measure the gloss of the floors for each aisle over several weeks for comparison. We used a digital gloss meter that provided numerical values for the shine on each aisle. Our product's gloss lasted longer, and we were able to prove that although we were more expensive initially, the stores used less floor product annually. We were successful, but we had to prove our value on a regular basis. We could prove that with longer durability and better performance, the customer had lower annual costs. No matter what industry you are in, customers need to understand the financial value you bring to their business.

Remember, a strong value proposition is essential for building trust and credibility. By focusing on the customer's needs and demonstrating how your solution can help them achieve their goals, you will increase your chance of closing sales.

DATA SPEAKS LOUDER THAN PERCEPTION

Early in my career, I took note of who were the most successful and respected sales professionals in my territory. One sales pro I observed worked for a chemical company and was particularly outstanding. Being in the same industry, we had several of the same accounts. Early in my career, he came into one of our customers carrying a large bag that contained the original Apple Macintosh computer. Very few people were collecting data to show value back then. Since he was the only representative with a Mac, I asked him what he was going to do with it. He mentioned that he needed to analyze data to document the value his products were bringing to the customer. He said, "Tim, data will always speak louder than perception." All these years later, I vividly remember that conversation. He knew the importance of using data to support the value story. Of course, today using data to support the value proposition is standard practice.

Our job is to prove value to our customers. A customer may think you are the nicest person they have ever met, but if you cannot bring value to their business, you will not likely gain many purchase orders.

Here are some strategies for crafting effective value propositions:

- Understand your customer needs: Uncover where the gap in satisfaction is with your customer and how your products can help.

- Quantify the value: Use data to demonstrate the monetary impact of your solution.

- Highlight unique benefits: Differentiate your offerings from competitors.

- Use case studies: These are highly effective to illustrate the value of your products or services.

- Create a clear and professional proposal that highlights the specific financial value of your product or service.

How does your product bring value to customers?

_____

_____

_____

_____

_____

What part of your customers' business can they expect to see a positive financial impact on by using your products (cost savings, increased production, quality improvement)?

_____

_____

_____

_____

_____

List two case studies in which customers have seen a positive financial impact using your products:

1._____

2._____

> *Treat objections as requests for further*
> *information.*
>
> —*Brian Tracey*

HANDLING OBJECTIONS

Objections are a natural part of the sales process. They often indicate that the customer is interested but needs additional information or reassurance. By anticipating and effectively addressing objections, you can build trust and increase your chances of closing sales.

It is more concerning if your potential customer does not have any feedback for you. There will be some objections you can solve and others that will be a challenge. Price will come up a lot as an objection. Anticipate this and be prepared to restate your value proposition. Do not be surprised or discouraged because a customer is pushing back. Be prepared by asking yourself all the possible objections that may come up before meeting with the customer.

Stay calm when objections get thrown at you. If you prepare properly, dealing with objections will go a lot better. The customer must know you take their objections seriously. Make sure you listen to their concerns and try to represent your company's and customer's best interests. Always acknowledge and respect their feedback.

Several years ago, I was making a sales call with one of our most experienced sales representatives at a key account. The customer was very informed and knowledgeable about his business. We were having a conversation about a technical aspect of our proposal, and the customer was throwing every objection he could our way. Our representative stayed calm and confident and effectively dealt with every objection the customer had. It was incredible to watch as both were highly capable at their jobs and had respectful disagreements. Our representative had built up a lot of trust and respect by having a clear understanding of the customer's operation and needs. Our sales associate had the technical experience and a strong relationship with the customer. This led to a productive and candid discussion. They did not agree on everything but came away with a great plan to work together. Their mutual respect created a great working relationship. The time our sales pro had spent building the relationship and understanding the customer's operation was evident throughout the discussion.

If you have a compelling value proposition, do not sell down to an inferior product if price is the main objection. You will be held accountable for your product's performance once the customer purchases it. Sometimes salespeople will change their product offering if price remains the main obstacle. You have proposed a product to provide a solution to your customer. Stick to your story, reinforce value, and try your best to represent both the customer and your company.

Here are some strategies for overcoming objections:

- Use your listening skills: Clearly understand the customer's perspective before responding.

- Empathize: Acknowledge the customer's concerns and show understanding.

- Be prepared by studying your proposal and anticipate objections.

- Focus on value: Reinforce the benefits of your product or service.

Remember, objections are not personal attacks. By managing them professionally and confidently, you can turn potential obstacles into opportunities for growth.

Common objections:

- You are too expensive!

  Example: Our customers have received outstanding value from our product solutions.

- We are not ready to commit!

  Example: We are ready to supply our solution when you are, but we are seeing excellent demand and want to make sure we can help you in a timely manner to improve your business.

- We are afraid of change and will stay with our existing supplier.

  Example: Progress means change. We respect and appreciate how you feel, but our goal is to help you win. We believe our value solution will help improve your business.

To effectively sell products to customers, we need to articulate our value story. The story needs to be backed up by facts that are relevant to the customer and their business. They may need to sell our proposal internally to other stakeholders, so preparing the customer with everything they need to tell the story is critical. Businesses are under pressure to perform, and the more clearly we can state our value story, the better our success rate will be.

Here are two objections I have heard from customers about my value proposals:

1._____

_____

2._____

_____

KEY TAKEAWAYS

1. Use financial metrics to support your value story.

2. Create a compelling value-based proposal for your customer.

3. Be prepared to handle every objection.

Rate yourself 1–10 on providing win-win solutions:

_____

Sales Separator #8—Follow Up!

Diligent follow-up and follow-through will set you apart from the crowd and communicate excellence.

—John C. Maxwell

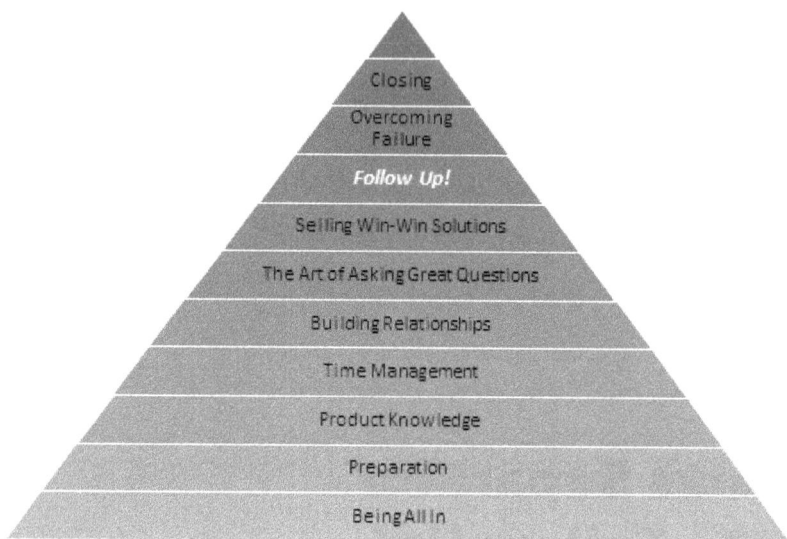

A sales professional who follows up promptly and consistently stands out. From my experience, at least 50 percent of salespeople do not excel in this critical area. Many salespeople will commit to following up, but you never hear from them again.

I find this amazing because of the negative impression it leaves on people. Why is this? I believe part of it is that some salespeople are not organized well enough and do not have a system for their follow-up. This lack of organization causes lost opportunities that affect sales revenue and the salesperson's reputation. Your reputation is so important, and references are always used in business. Following up promptly will get you a positive recommendation from people and more opportunities to grow your business. Even if you do not have all the answers, it is important for people to know you are thinking about them. Excellent follow-up leads to confidence with buyers making major decisions. Your follow-up practices need to separate you from the competition and are essential for sales success. Your customers are busy, and you are competing for their attention; make sure you stand out by communicating with them professionally.

Most sales opportunities go through a buying cycle that requires multiple interactions with people. Rarely does a complex sale happen after just a few contacts. It is vital that you keep the communication moving forward with prospects and customers to progress the sales process.

When you commit to a customer about getting back to them regarding expected delivery, quotes, or other information, you are making a promise. This also applies to people you work with internally. If you say you are going to do something, you are responsible for making it happen. People are gauging you based on how you keep your promises. Your response must be timely, based on the expectation you have set with people. If you commit to responding to people within twenty-four hours, then that is what is required. Depending on the information needed, set a realistic expectation with people on when you will follow up with them.

Poor follow-up sets the tone for the service customers can expect in the future. I expect people to get back to me quickly, even if they do not have all the information. I need to know they are working on my behalf and are interested in helping me. It is frustrating for people to be left wondering what is happening in business situations. It does not take a lot of effort to stay in touch. When I find someone who follows up promptly, I find reasons to do more business with them, and your customers and prospects are no different.

Following up immediately will show how professional you are and how much you care about a customer's business. To be successful, you must respond to customers with urgency. Be known as the sales pro who follows up the best in your industry. Part of your weekly plan should include a list of key follow-ups and people who need to be contacted. Always be known as someone who is a step ahead of the competition and always have your customers' best interests at heart. Let your customers know how important they are to you and your company. Providing outstanding follow-up is mandatory to be the best.

Most complex sales take a lot of communication over time and involve a series of exchanges with people. Several years ago, we had a key meeting at the corporate headquarters of a major customer to discuss a long-term contract. Our team had been working for months on putting together a proposal to supply their global operations. The meeting went well, but there were some timely follow-ups that needed to be addressed quickly. Instead of returning to the hotel to work, we asked the customer if we could use one of the conference rooms at their headquarters so we could get to work immediately. It worked out great as the conference room had a glass wall where the customer could see us working throughout the day. They even touched base with us during the day to see if we needed input from them. We were able to focus as a team and follow up immediately on their questions and had everything back to them by the end of the day. Most of the items were agreed upon, and we came away with a solid plan to work together. They knew how important the relationship was to us, and we showed it by our response that day.

Early in my career, one of my largest accounts called me on New Year's Day from their manufacturing operation. They were running out of a critical material we supplied them, and they would have to shut down their operation if we did not deliver more product within the next few days. Our manufacturing site was several states away, and getting trucks for delivery over the New Year's holiday was particularly challenging. The account's leadership was on a speaker call with me, and together we immediately went to work. Although it was a holiday, I was able to communicate with our transportation resources and schedule immediate deliveries. We worked throughout the day together and were successful in keeping the account supplied when they needed help. They were very relieved and appreciative that our product would get there without any interruption in their manufacturing process. I vividly remember a meeting about a year later at the customer site when the competition was making a pitch to gain our business. The executive responsible for the site said, "Will the new company be there for us on New Year's Day?" I am proud to say we kept the business.

Here are some effective follow-up strategies:

- Have a daily follow-up list: Use a system to organize your key commitments for responding to people.

- Set an agreed-upon time with people when they can expect to hear back from you.

- Document your sales calls in CRM or another system that can help track follow-up.

- Keep working on your customer's behalf by communicating their questions and concerns internally.

- Make sure your customers know you are thinking about them with frequent communication.

Remember, follow-up is not about being pushy; it is about providing excellent customer service and demonstrating your commitment to helping customers succeed. Great follow-up will separate you from the competition and give people the confidence to do business with you.

KEY TAKEAWAYS

1. Make following up with urgency a top priority.

2. Use great follow-up to separate you from the competition.

3. Keep in close touch with customers even if you do not have all the answers.

Rate yourself 1–10 on following up:

_____

Here is my plan to improve my follow-up:

_____

_____

_____

_____

_____

_____

Sales Separator #9—Overcoming Failure

*It's not about how hard you fail: it's about
how you rise back up*

—Dan Gable

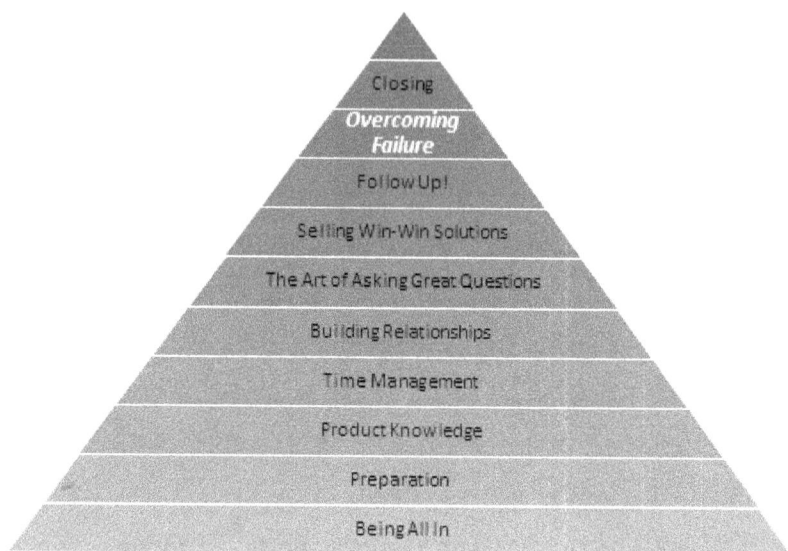

We all experience failure at some point. The ability to rebound from failure is one of the greatest separators of outstanding sales professionals. As I reflect on my favorite sports legends, they all dealt with failure at some point, learned from it, and became great champions.

Early in my career, I had a very challenging period when success was hard to come by for several reasons. A lot of effort was going into selling new opportunities, but I was not successful enough to convince customers to change from their existing suppliers. I was working hard but not seeing any increase in my sales or my income. There was no choice but to regroup and keep going. It can be frustrating and discouraging to work hard and not obtain the results we want.

Your ability to bounce back and keep fighting on despite major setbacks is the grit you need to succeed. No one is successful all the time. In your business, there will be sales that go to competitors, lost business because of issues beyond your control, and other unforeseen setbacks. This happens to everyone. I had a flat tire in a customer parking lot after they told me I had lost their business! This day had gone so badly for me that I just had to laugh changing the tire.

At one point on my sales team, our success rate needed improvement with our new product opportunities. We were effectively selling the potential value of the product but not executing when we had the opportunity to implement with customers. We found we were spending more time on postmortem meetings trying to figure out what happened after failures than on effective planning going into a project. One of my customers introduced me to the book *Flawless Execution: Use the Techniques and Systems of America's Fighter Pilots to Perform at Your Peak and Win the Battles of the Business World* by James D. Murphy. The book describes the "Plan-Brief-Execute-Debrief-Win" cycle and highlights the importance of effective planning and communication before, during, and after fighter pilot combat missions. This resonated with our team as we were not devoting enough time to pre-project execution and not conducting post-project debriefings.

As the book suggests, we began to implement meetings with everyone involved in the execution of a major sales project before and after the execution phase. We used these meetings to go over every detail we could think of so we would not be surprised when we implemented our products. No project goes exactly as planned, but my experience is that if we are talking about a potential issue, at least we will not be surprised.

By using the briefing method and other practices from the book, we were able to increase our product success rate. Our planning was better, and a lot less time was spent troubleshooting because we were so much more prepared going into projects. We were also learning from the post-implementation briefings. Most importantly, our customers benefited from better planning and execution.

In Roger Federer's commencement speech at Dartmouth College, he said that although he won almost 80 percent of the 1,526 matches throughout his career, he won only 54 percent of the points he played. One of the greatest of all time won just over half the points he played. In the speech he said, "You want to become the master of overcoming hard moments. That is the sign of a champion. The best know they will lose again and again and have learned how to deal with it."[20] The most important points are always the next ones.

Even Tom Brady said "You guys know how many times I have been turned down in my life? To be told how many times that I could not accomplish something?"[21] Brady used the doubters and negative feedback to fuel his desire to win. He elevated everyone around him to be their best.

It is difficult to lose business or have major deals go to competitors. I had my share of disappointments early on and took those defeats harder than I should have. As I became more experienced, I realized that every situation is a learning opportunity. The longer you stay in the game, the more effective and strategic you become. You learn there will be other opportunities, and you work harder to win each time. The key is to think long term, improve your skills, and prepare for the next opportunity.

NEVER PLAY THE BLAME GAME

There will be sales situations in which you believe you should have succeeded but did not. Defeat can come from many different things, but it is essential to always be supportive of your company and the people you work with. Our job as sales leaders is to take responsibility for the results whether we win or lose. The best test of our character is when things are most challenging. We always need to be loyal to the company we work for and the people who are helping us. Everyone can handle winning; it is how we handle and rebound from defeat that defines us. As sales leaders, we own the results.

NEVER QUIT

Many times, success will come after we have major setbacks. We must keep going and persevere over the long run even as we face defeat. One situation was particularly disappointing and deflating for me. It involved a big project with a key customer that would have yielded a large increase in sales, but it was not successful. This opportunity with the customer was years in the making, and I had been optimistic we would gain the business. We all worked very hard on the project, but our proposed product did not help the customer as we expected. The customer quickly went back to their existing supplier. Because the stakes were high, I knew it would be quite a while before I was granted another opportunity.

It was a long ride home from the customer site, and I did a lot of thinking. I decided it was time to work on a very different project for a few days over the weekend. My wife and I had been thinking about building a swing in our yard for our girls. I headed to the store, bought the supplies we needed, and started building between two big trees. It turned out great, and we all used that swing the entire time we lived there. The swing is still there today, and I know exactly the day it was built. Sometimes we just need to take a break, work on something else, and start over. Quitting is never an option.

PERSEVERANCE WILL PUSH YOU TO THE TOP

So many of the successful business situations I was involved with came after significant setbacks. You will find that if you keep pursuing your objectives and putting forth your best effort, success will eventually come your way. From sales success to job promotions, things rarely go exactly as planned. There were occasions when I pursued positions of greater responsibility and did not get the promotions. Each of these situations gave me more time to prepare by focusing on improving my skill set for future career opportunities. As it turned out, not getting promoted at times was a gift that enabled me to focus on what I would need in the future to be a better leader. By thinking long term and using defeat as a learning opportunity, you will become more effective. Your determination will push you through to a place where you will experience victory.

Recommendations on dealing with setbacks:

- Do not overreact to setbacks. Easier said than done, but when failure comes, stay calm, assess, and regroup.

- Do not play the blame game. Take ownership of results.

- Take a break and work on something else. This could be a home project, a hobby, or just taking a breather from your job.

- Remember: to be the best in anything, you need to be able to power through.

- Take a few minutes and write down what you are grateful for. This will put a work project into perspective.

- Even in your major wins, always remain humble. Hit your home runs and run the bases with your head down.

Remember, you are all in through good times and bad. Now come up with a new plan, regroup, and get back to work!

KEY TAKEAWAYS

1. Learn from setbacks and constantly improve.

2. Prepare for the marathon. A sales career is a long-term effort.

3. Recharge, regroup, and forge ahead.

Rate yourself 1–10 on overcoming failure:

_____

Here are two situations where I displayed resiliency:

1._____

_____

_____

_____

_____

2._____

_____

_____

_____

_____

Sales Separator #10—Closing

You get nothing you do not ask for.

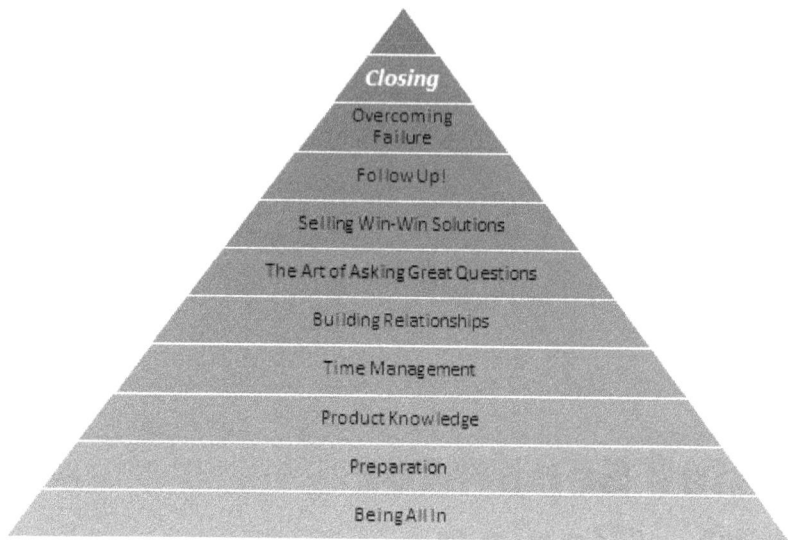

Professional closing is the culmination of the sales process. It is the moment when you transform a prospect into a customer. While it can be nerve racking, a confident and well-executed close is essential for sales success.

You have done all the work to prepare and present a great win-win value solution. A lot of time and effort has gone into building the relationship, asking great questions to uncover the gap in satisfaction, and delivering a solid proposal. Why are some salespeople afraid to ask for the order?

One of the reasons is tension. Asking for the order can make us feel uncomfortable because the customer may say no, and we do not want to be let down. We may be fearful we might come on too strong in asking for the order and damage the relationship. Between being afraid of rejection and avoiding the tension of asking for the order, so many opportunities get lost. The customer is waiting for us to ask for the order!

You cannot come across as pushy or arrogant, but a well-rehearsed close can help ease the tension that may potentially arise. Never apply pressure when asking for the business. Remember, you are a consultant helping them solve their problems. The entire sales process has led to this point when you can confidently stand by your value proposal and ask for the order. If you have addressed all the customer objections, then you are ready to ask about obtaining a purchase order. Helping the customer understand how to place an order with your company is key. How orders are placed, who should they contact, timing of delivery, and method of delivery need to be communicated.

Make it easy for your customers to do business with you and your company. Communicate how their order will be managed and how you will let them know every step of the way when they can expect delivery. I would ask, "Making sure we give you our best delivery and service, can we place an order as soon as possible so we can get you in line to receive the product?"

The customer may still have some major objections. There may still be some significant areas of disagreement. In situations like this, I try and put myself in their position and do what I believe is fair. Many times, we are negotiating not just with the customer but with our own company as well. Creating a small win or concession for a potential customer to help move the business your way is not uncommon. These concessions should not be so large that the buyer questions why you have changed your original proposal. Small concessions can be symbolic of letting the buyer have a win to obtain the business. Most people do not like change, so a small initial incentive may be needed to move the process along. Major reductions in price reduce your product's value and affect the credibility of your story. If price is still the focus of the conversation, then the value story has not resonated.

Your customer may need time to decide, which is fine. Purchasing a different product or service may take additional analysis on their part. Follow up professionally and give them the space they need to make a thoughtful business decision.

If you do not get the order, it is not fatal. Act professionally and tell them that you appreciate the opportunity to propose your solution. Let them know you will continue to connect with them, and they can contact you with any questions. If your solution is sound, you will likely get an opportunity in the future.

Here are some closing techniques to consider:

- Summarize your value story: Recap the key benefits and value proposition before asking for the order. Look for affirmation from the customer that they understand what you are proposing.

- Have logistics worked out in advance: Check on delivery dates, product availability, or other areas that might be important regarding the order.

- Let the customer know you are confident about your proposal: This will help build assurance with the customer and their decision.

- Ask permission to move forward. If everyone agrees on the product or solution, it is time to process the purchase order.

- Always be polite and respectful and never pushy. The relationship is too important.

Remember, the best closing technique is the one that feels natural and authentic. Practice and preparation are paramount to effectively obtaining purchase orders. By building rapport, understanding your customers' needs, and delivering an exceptional value story, you'll increase your chances for a successful close.

Always thank a potential customer for the opportunity to present your value proposal!

Here are two ways I will ask for the order:

1._____

_____

_____

_____

_____

2._____

_____

_____

_____

_____

IF YOU DO NOT GET THE BUSINESS, FIND OUT WHY

Losing a sale to the competition can be very disappointing, but it is also an opportunity to learn and improve. We need to understand the reasons a customer decided to choose a competitive offering. This feedback can help refine our sales approach and increase our chances of success in the future. It never feels good to have the business go to a competitor, but we need to make sure we understand what we could have done better so we can improve.

One great sales pro I worked with had lost a major piece of business because of a strong relationship the buyer had with a competitor. As hard as he worked to get the business back by bringing value to the customer, orders still went to the competition. One day, the key decision-maker complimented our sales associate on the great work he had been doing to help their operation. Our professional was not obtaining purchase orders but was still working hard to help the customer's operation. Our sales pro responded to the customer, "If you feel that strongly about the value my service is providing, I would also like to show you our newest product offering to help your operation. Can you place a purchase order so that we can deliver the product quickly and show you the immediate benefits?" The customer agreed and placed the order. Our sales pro got his product back on the customer's machine, provided value, and eventually won all the business back. This was a fitting example of great follow-up, providing outstanding value, and asking for the business.

Here are some strategies for handling lost sales:

- Request feedback: Politely ask the customer their reasons for choosing a competitor. Respect their decision.

- Conduct a post-sale analysis: Review the sales process to identify things that went well or could have been improved on.

- Share insights with your team: Everyone can learn and improve.

- Maintain a positive attitude: View lost sales as opportunities for growth and development.

Remember, every lost sale is a chance to improve. By embracing feedback and making necessary adjustments, you will continue to improve.

KEY TAKEAWAYS

1. You get nothing you do not ask for. Ask professionally for the order.

2. Be prepared to restate your value story.

3. Thank the customer for the opportunity.

Rate yourself 1–10 on closing effectiveness:

What Does Success Look Like?

*If one advances confidently in the direction
of his dreams, and endeavors to live the life
which he has imagined, he will meet with a
success unexpected in common hours*

—Henry David Thoreau

Success means different things to different people. It is important to define your own version of success to create a clear vision for your life and career. By having a clear picture of success, you can focus your energy on achieving it.

Imagine yourself successful. Is it financial freedom, professional recognition, work-life balance, personal growth, or something else entirely? Your definition of success might change over time, and that is perfectly fine.

As Stephen R. Covey wrote, "You don't want to climb the ladder of success and, upon reaching the top rung, realize that the ladder is leaning against the wrong wall."[22] We need to understand what success looks like to each of us.

Think about people you have known in your life who you believe are successful. What attributes do they have? The successful people I have known are committed to their families and their jobs, take care of themselves, and are optimistic about the future. Successful people I have known are interested in other people. They reach out and are curious about how friends and colleagues are doing. They are not in this life for just themselves. They often ask, "How can I help you?" and "How are you doing?" Another important trait is that successful people exhibit humility and do not take themselves too seriously.

I recently started swimming for fitness and do it consistently. I swam year-round on swim teams as a kid and did not enjoy it. My brother was an excellent swimmer, and I tagged along at the practices and competitions. Doing laps in the pool is great exercise, and when we were in Maine visiting family this past summer, I thought ocean swimming would be even better than a pool. Our daughter lives near the coast, so getting access to cold salt water was convenient. I bought a wet suit, and off I went without a clue of what I was doing. I luckily found and joined a group of experienced ocean swimmers, and they quickly showed me I had better stay humble in the ocean and not take myself too seriously. The first time I swam with them, I put my wet suit on backward, and the next time inside out. All we could do was laugh. I quickly learned that swimming in the ocean required an entirely new level of skill, grit, and knowledge: a humbling experience that pushed me out of my comfort zone and made me want to continue to improve.

Remember, success is a journey, not a destination. Celebrate your milestones along the way, and do not hesitate to redefine success as your life progresses. Take a few minutes to think about who you believe is successful and your own vision of what success looks like to you.

Here are two examples of people I believe are successful and why:

1._____

_____

_____

_____

2._____

_____

_____

_____

Success to me looks like:

_____

_____

_____

_____

_____

_____

_____

Having Goals Is Essential

The thing about goals is that living without
them is a lot more fun, in the short run.
It seems to me, though, that the people who
get things done, who lead, who grow and
who make an impact . . . those people
have goals.

—*Seth Godin*

Having written goals will sharpen your focus. What are your top three for your business? Studies have shown the powerful effect that writing goals down has on accomplishing them. Research indicates that roughly 3 percent of people have goals that are written down. Great sales pros set goals and put plans in place to achieve them. Ask people you know if they have a set of written goals. The answer will surprise you.

Setting goals has always been crucial for me. Whether in sports or business, goals provided me with clear objectives. I have challenged people who complained about their jobs about what their top three goals were. Many had no goals to focus their energy on. Without goals to guide us, we can easily find ourselves drifting unproductively.

As Richard Koch writes in the book *The 80/20 Principle*, "People who write down their goals and review them frequently are much more likely to attain them. It is a separate question whether or not you should set goals for yourself. This is what I think: Goals are great if you want to make a dent in the cosmos, if you are interested in extraordinary achievement, or if you want to make a lot of money."[23] Writing goals down creates a new level of focus.

I was speaking with an industry colleague many years ago who was complaining about everything. This included his company, the industry, and even his customers. After listening to his set of grievances, I asked him what his top three goals were, and he looked at me, shocked that I would even ask. He said he did not have any. At that point, I suggested this would be a great place for him to start. He eventually thought about our conversation and put together his top three. Every time I would see him after that, he would mention his top three goals and challenge me on what mine were. I must admit he did catch me a few times reaching for an answer. It was amazing to see the impact that writing his goals down had on his attitude, outlook, and happiness.

Writing down your goals is a powerful way to clarify your focus and create a road map for success. When you write down your goals on paper, you make a personal commitment. I genuinely believe that if you have worthy goals and work hard to attain them, the universe conspires to help you. Using your imagination to visualize what you are trying to achieve can be highly effective in beginning the process of realizing your aspirations. Going for a walk and thinking about what you want to achieve can be a productive way to exercise and allow your mind to focus. I like to start my day with a meditative walk so I can peacefully think about the important priorities I need to work on.

CONSIDER THE SMART METHOD FOR YOUR GOALS

A helpful method for setting and achieving goals was originally proposed by George T. Doran using the acronym SMART. By utilizing this technique, you can provide structure to each of your goals.

- **Specific:** Clearly state the objective.

- **Measurable:** How will progress be tracked?

- **Achievable:** Must be realistic.

- **Relevant:** Aligned with strategy.

- **Time-Bound:** Have a realistic time period.

Remember, goals are not set in stone. Regularly review and adjust your goals as needed to stay on track. I have known people who completely transformed their sales performance by setting goals. We should always be ready when someone asks us what our top three are.

CONSIDER KEEPING A JOURNAL

Throughout my career, writing in a journal has been a great way to express ideas, track progress, and put my thoughts down on paper. It is a productive way to empty your thoughts so you can free up mental space for creative thinking. This has been helpful in my career in setting goals, monitoring progress, and documenting my thoughts. As you look back on your notes, you will likely see patterns that will be helpful to see how you assessed things at different times. When you journal over time, your thought patterns provide insight into how you think and make decisions. I recommend you try this practice, and hopefully it will prove helpful.

What are your three SMART business goals for the next ninety days?

1._____

2._____

3._____

Putting It All Together

Don't measure yourself by what you have accomplished, but by what you should have accomplished with your ability.

—John Wooden

Hopefully, this book is full of your notes and action plans. We started with the importance of what motivates and is meaningful to you. *You are in charge of where you go from here.* We have covered the ten Sales Separators to compete and win. By consistently applying these principles, you will develop the skills, mindset, and strategies needed to achieve outstanding, sustainable results.

Someone recently asked me what the "it" factor is in great sales pros. I reflected on it and said it all comes back to motivation. Being highly motivated is the starting point for a successful sales career. If someone is motivated and willing to learn, they can be successful.

You are a committed sales professional who has taken charge of your professional development and has the initiative to be the best you can be. You have already proven you are highly motivated by working on your sales skill development. You are all in. With a clear understanding of your core values, you are ready to take on your sales career in a way that matches what is truly meaningful to you. You now have a vision of what success looks like and understand the importance of setting SMART business goals.

We covered the importance of preparation and putting plans in place to learn about your industry, your company, and the customers in your territory. Having great mentors will help you learn and grow throughout your career. Success begins with preparation.

Becoming a product expert and learning everything you can about what you sell and the value it can bring to customers will help separate you from the competition. You have a plan to enhance your product knowledge that will pay dividends and enable you to provide customers with effective solutions. Product expertise gives customers the confidence to do business with you.

Time management is a priority and will lead to better results by focusing on the areas and customers that will provide the best return. Applying the 80/20 principle will help you be more effective at planning your time and increase your effectiveness by focusing on areas that will have the largest impact. We are as good as how we spend our time.

Establishing key relationships is the foundation for your success. Working to always keep your relationships above neutral is paramount. Recognizing people for the great work they do will help you build a culture of teamwork. You have listed your top ten contacts and have a plan to build those relationships. Skills get you started, but relationships will make your career.

Honing your ability to ask great questions will lead to a better understanding of people and the problems they face. Uncovering the gap in satisfaction with customers will provide the opportunity to create win-win solutions. Remember, everyone is unhappy about something in their business.

Providing outstanding value solutions will give you the ability to help customers solve issues and improve their business. Delivering a well-crafted value story will give customers the confidence to move business your way. Data speaks louder than perception.

Following up with urgency will separate you from your competitors. This will make you stand out as a true professional, and customers will appreciate your responsiveness. Always let your customers know you are thinking about them.

Being able to overcome failure will help you navigate the difficulties we all experience in a sales career. You know a successful sales career is a marathon and not a sprint. Never give up.

Professionally asking customers for their business will help you close and win more sales. If you do not gain the opportunity, remember you need to learn from it and improve. You will get nothing you do not ask for.

You put this all together, and you are ready to sell to win!

Remember, success in a sales career is a journey, not a destination. Continuously seek opportunities for growth, learning, and improvement. Stay committed to your goals, and never stop believing in your ability to succeed.

With dedication, perseverance, and a relentless pursuit of excellence, you can become a top professional in your industry. It is time to unleash your full potential.

Reference each chapter and look at what you have written down. The notes, ideas, and action plans that you have developed can help you on your path to success.

The last recommendation in this book is to review how you rated yourself on each of the ten principles and input the data in the summary sheet. As you look at your ratings, you can see the areas that need potential improvement. My hope is that this proves useful to you and your development.

I wish you happiness in your life and success in your sales career.

Summary of ratings for the Sales Separators:

- Being all in _____

- Preparation _____

- Product knowledge _____

- Time management _____

- Building relationships _____

- Asking great questions _____

- Selling win-win solutions _____

- Follow up! _____

- Overcoming failure _____

- Closing _____

- Total _____

Based on my ratings for the Sales Separators, here is my action plan to be my best:

1._____

2._____

3._____

4._____

5._____

6._____

7._____

8._____

9._____

10._____

Acknowledgements

Sincere gratitude to my family for listening to my stories and supporting me during the writing of this book. You were my motivation to win in my sales career.

Thanks to the great customers over my career that provided the opportunity to provide value and challenged me to grow and improve.

To my mentors that pushed me to improve and provided the feedback and opportunities that were so important for my career growth. My sales mentors Don Earl and Dick Brennan, who provided me with the path to get started. My management mentors Bubba Livingston and Tom Durkin. You provided the opportunity and guidance for me to learn and grow as a leader.

To the great sales professionals on the teams that I worked in. I learned something from all of you.

To Chris, Todd, John, and Ken for your feedback especially in the early stages of writing this book.

Many thanks to Shilah, Kathy, and the Bublish publishing team for being instrumental in helping me complete this book.

Bibliography

Blanchard, Ken. n.d. *https://www.azquotes.com/author/ 1497-Ken_Blanchard.*

Brady, Tom. 2023. *Top 23 Tom Brady's Inspirational Quotes Of All Time!* Motiversity.

Burkeman, Oliver. 2021. *TIme Management for Mortals .* New York: Farrar, Straus, and Giroux.

Carnegie, Dale. n.d. *https://www.azquotes.com/quote/ 48701.*

Clayton M. Christianson, James Allworth, Karen Dillon. 2012. *How Will Meaure Your Life?* New York: HarperCollins.

Covey, Steven R. 1989. *The 7 Habits Of Highly Effective People.* New York: SIMON & SCHUSTER.

Deming, W. Edwards. n.d. *https://en.wikiquote.org/wiki/W._Edwards_Deming.*

Diviney, Rich. 2021. *The Attributes.* New York: Random House.

Drucker, Peter. 2006. *The Effectiive Executive* . New York: HarperCollins.

Einstein. n.d. *https://www.socratic-method.com/quote-meanings/albert-einstein-if-you-cant-explain-it-simply-you-dont-understand-it-well-enough.*

Federer, Roger. 2024. "Dartmouth Commencement Speech."

Fuller, Ryan. 2015. "3 Behaviors That Drive Successful Salespeople." *Harvard Business Review.*

Gable, Dan. n.d. *https://burningforsuccess.com/dan-gable-quotes/.*

Gladwell, Malcolm. 2000. *THe TIPPING POINT.* New York: Little, Brown, and Company.

Godin, Seth. 2010. *LINCHPIN.* New York: Simon & Schuster.

GODIN, SETH. 2018. *THIS IS MARKETING.* New York: Porfolio/Penguin.

Koch, RIchard. 2017. *The 80/20 Principle.* New York: Penguin Random House.

Leonard, George. 1991. *MASTERY.* New York: Penguin Group.

Martin, Steven W. 2015. "What Separates the Strongest Salespeople from the Weakest." *Harvard Business Review.*

Maxwell, John. n.d. *https://sourcesofinsight.com/john-maxwell-quotes/.*

Murphy, James D. 2005. *Flawless Execution.* New York: HarperCollins.

Rackham, Neil. 1989. *MAJOR ACCOUNT SALES STRATEGY.* Baskerville: McGraw-Hill.

Rohn, Jim. n.d. *https://www.goodreads.com/quotes/42751-motivation-is-what-gets-you-started-habit-is-what-keeps.*

Seneca. n.d. *https://www.azquotes.com/author/1497-Ken_Blanchard.*

Thoreau, Henry David. n.d. *https://www.goodreads.com/quotes/290603-if-one-advances-confidently-in-the-direction-of-his-dreams.*

Twain, Mark. n.d. *I can live for two months on a good compliment.* Brainy Quote.

Ziglar, Zig. n.d. *https://mindfuldevmag.com/newsletter/lack-of-direction-not-lack-of-time-is-the-problem.*

Endnotes

1. Steven W. Martin, "What Separates the Strongest Salespeople from the Weakest." Harvard Business Review Digital Article. March 18, 2015. http://hbsp.harvard/product/Ho1Y4F

2. Steven W. Martin, "What Separates the Strongest Salespeople from the Weakest." Harvard Business Review Digital Article. March 18, 2015. http://hbsp.harvard/product/Ho1Y4F

3. Steven W. Martin, "What Separates the Strongest Salespeople from the Weakest." Harvard Business Review Digital Article. March 18, 2015. http://hbsp.harvard/product/Ho1Y4F

4. Diviney, Rich. The Attributes. New York: Random House, 2021. Page 59.

5. Covey, Steven R. The 7 Habits Of Highly Effective People. New York: Simon & Schuster, 1989. Page 99.

6. Fuller, Ryan. "3 Behaviors That Drive Successful Salespeople." Harvard Business Review, 2015. 3 Behaviors That Drive Successful Salespeople

7. Fuller, Ryan. "3 Behaviors That Drive Successful Salespeople." Harvard Business Review, 2015. 3 Behaviors That Drive Successful Salespeople

8. Fuller, Ryan. "3 Behaviors That Drive Successful Salespeople." Harvard Business Review, 2015. 3 Behaviors That Drive Successful Salespeople

9. Clayton M. Christianson, James Allworth, Karen Dillon. How Will You Measure Your Life? New York: HarperCollins, 2012.

10. Godin, Seth. Linchpin. New York: Simon & Schuster, 2010.

11. Rackham, Neil. Major Account Sales Strategy. Baskerville: McGraw-Hill, 1989. Page 39.

12. Godin, Seth. This Is Marketing. New York: Portfolio/Penguin, 2018. Page 65.

13. Burkeman, Oliver. TIme Management for Mortals. New York: Farrar, Straus, and Giroux, 2021. Page 4.

14. Koch, Richard. The 80/20 Principle. New York: Penguin Random House, 2017. Page 4.

15. Drucker, Peter. The Effective Executive. New York: HarperCollins, 2006.Page 25.

16. Godin, Seth. Linchpin. New York: Simon & Schuster, 2010.

17. Mark Twain, "Letter to Gertrude Natkin," March 2, 1906. Per http://www.twainquotes.com

18. Drucker, Peter. The Effective Executive. New York: HarperCollins, 2006. Introduction.

19. Rackham, Neil. Major Account Sales Strategy. Baskerville: McGraw-Hill, 1989. Page 26.

20. Rackham, Neil. Major Account Sales Strategy. Baskerville: McGraw-Hill, 1989. Page 83, 84.

21. Federer, Roger. "Dartmouth Commencement Speech," 2024.

22. Brady, Tom.. Top 23 Tom Brady's Inspirational Quotes Of All Time! Motiversity, 2023.

23. Covey, Steven R. The 7 Habits Of Highly Effective People. New York: Simon & Schuster, 1989. Page 160.

24. Koch, Richard. The 80/20 Principle. New York: Penguin Random House, 2017. Page 243.

www.ingramcontent.com/pod-product-compliance
Lightning Source LLC
Chambersburg PA
CBHW071423210326
41597CB00020B/3627